QUICK WIN PRESENTATIONS

Answers to your top 100 presentation questions

2nd edition

Elizabeth P Tierney

·OAK·TREE·PRESS·

Published by OAK TREE PRESS, CORK T12 XY2N, IRELAND

www.oaktreepress.com / www.SuccessStore.com

© 2023 Elizabeth Tierney

A catalogue record of this book is available from the British Library.

ISBN 978 1 78119 610 6 (Paperback)
ISBN 978 1 78119 611 3 (PDF)
ISBN 978 1 78119 612 0 (ePub)
ISBN 978 1 78119 613 7 (Kindle)

INTRODUCTION

If asked to name our greatest fear in doing business, many of us would admit that we are most terrified at the notion of having to speak before a group. But it is often an essential part of our work. We give talks of one kind or another frequently. In a single week, a businessperson may be called upon to speak to the Board of Directors on Monday, to 10 colleagues at a department meeting on Tuesday morning, to 50 interested investors on Wednesday, to their personal staff of three remotely on Thursday, to a hiring panel on Friday or to an audience of 300 at a conference held at a hotel on Saturday. That's six presentations. Your list is undoubtedly longer.

Because speaking in public can be an unnerving experience, **QUICK WIN PRESENTATIONS** is written to help you decrease some of the anxiety that you are feeling, as well as to offer tips and techniques for enhancing your talks. To do that, the book examines the process from beginning to end and offers answers to your top 100 presentation questions.

QUICK WIN PRESENTATIONS is designed to break the process into parts, thus enabling you to search for the answers to your key questions. The better you understand, the more confident, credible and effective you will be as a speaker and the better able you will be to influence others, to demonstrate your talent, and to represent your organization.

There are five sections to this book:

- **Presentation Essentials** covers some of the fundamental questions that all speakers have about what makes an effective speaker, what is involved in the communication process, the importance of understanding and keeping your focus on the audience and on having a clear message.

- **Developing a Presentation** addresses the design of a speech or talk itself. Specifically, this section answers questions about the importance of having a strong opening, logical middle and powerful closing.

- **Presentation Tips & Techniques** answers questions ranging from word choices to aspects of verbal and non-verbal language. It also includes topics like handling your nerves, knowing the venue, preparing for questions and designing visuals.

- **On the Day** looks at the last-minute details and your emotions.

- **Afterwards** offers suggestions for your ongoing development as a speaker.

QUICK WIN PRESENTATIONS is designed so that you can dip in and out, seeking answers to your top presentation questions as they arise. Answers to your queries can be located not only from the contents list but also by using the subject grid at the start of the book and by following the thread of cross-references provided at the end of each Q&A.

The questions asked and answered in this book include questions I have encountered time and again from businesspeople over many years through my consulting and training work. I hope you find the book helpful.

Elizabeth P Tierney
Portland, OR
June 2023

CONTENTS

Search by theme:

Or search by topic:

Audience

Barriers

Delivery

Feedback

Message

Planning

Props

using the grid overleaf.

PRESENTATION ESSENTIALS	Audience	Barriers	Delivery	Feedback	Message	Planning	Props	Page
Q1 What makes an effective speaker?		☑	☑		☑	☑		2
Q2 What are the steps in the communication process?			☑	☑	☑	☑		4
Q3 What can prevent communication?	☑	☑	☑		☑	☑		6
Q4 How can I identify and eliminate my weaknesses as a speaker?	☑	☑	☑	☑		☑		8
Q5 What are my strengths as a speaker?		☑	☑					10
Q6 How important is understanding the audience?	☑				☑	☑		11
Q7 What do I need to know about the audience?	☑		☑			☑	☑	12
Q8 Who should I address my talk to?	☑		☑			☑		14
Q9 Why is the audience attending my talk?	☑	☑						15
Q10 How can I benefit from analyzing the relationships among the audience members?	☑					☑		16
Q11 What is the message of my talk?					☑	☑		18
Q12 What is the purpose of my talk?	☑				☑	☑		19
Q13 How can I anticipate objections to my message?	☑			☑		☑		20

PRESENTATION ESSENTIALS	Audience	Barriers	Delivery	Feedback	Message	Planning	Props	Page
Q14 What should I eliminate as I prepare my presentation?			☑		☑	☑		21
Q15 What approach to the subject should I choose?			☑			☑		22

DEVELOPING A PRESENTATION	Audience	Barriers	Delivery	Feedback	Message	Planning	Props	Page
Q16 How important is the audience's first impression of a speaker?	☑		☑				☑	24
Q17 What motivational techniques can I use to grab the audience's attention?	☑		☑				☑	25
Q18 Why is it important to state my purpose?	☑		☑		☑			26
Q19 What value is there in explaining my format?	☑		☑					27
Q20 How should I organize the body of my talk?			☑			☑		28
Q21 Is using numbers a useful organizing structure?			☑			☑		30
Q22 Is using chronology a useful organizing structure?			☑			☑		31

DEVELOPING A PRESENTATION	Audience	Barriers	Delivery	Feedback	Message	Planning	Props	Page
Q23 Is order of importance a useful organizing structure?			☑			☑		32
Q24 Are mnemonics a useful organizing structure?			☑			☑		33
Q25 Is it wrong to repeat information?			☑					34
Q26 When is it useful to locate information by clarifying spatial relations?			☑			☑		35
Q27 How can I conclude a talk effectively?			☑			☑		36
Q28 How should I handle courtesies like "thank you"?			☑			☑		38

PRESENTATION TIPS & TECHNIQUES	Audience	Barriers	Delivery	Feedback	Message	Planning	Props	Page
Q29 Should I avoid jargon and colloquialisms?		☑	☑					40
Q30 Should I explain technical language?		☑	☑					41
Q31 Am I aware of my verbal idiosyncrasies?		☑	☑					42
Q32 Should I read my paper?		☑	☑					43

PRESENTATION TIPS & TECHNIQUES	Audience	Barriers	Delivery	Feedback	Message	Planning	Props	Page
Q47 How rapidly should I speak?		☑	☑			☑		60
Q48 How does altering the volume of my voice motivate the audience?			☑				☑	61
Q49 How can I discover whether I make unnecessary sounds when I speak?		☑	☑					62
Q50 Should I change my personality when I speak?			☑					67
Q51 What is the power of pausing?			☑			☑		64
Q52 Why is enthusiasm essential?			☑					65
Q53 Is stage fright normal?		☑	☑					66
Q54 How can I handle my own nervous reactions?			☑					67
Q55 How should I handle mistakes and surprises?		☑	☑					69
Q56 Are there proven ways to stay calm?			☑					70
Q57 How can I build my confidence as a speaker?	☑		☑			☑		71
Q58 Why is it important to get to know the layout of the venue?		☑	☑			☑	☑	72
Q59 Should I use a microphone?		☑	☑			☑	☑	74

PRESENTATION TIPS & TECHNIQUES	Audience	Barriers	Delivery	Feedback	Message	Planning	Props	Page
Q60 What kind of set up do I need to ensure a smooth presentation?		☑	☑			☑	☑	75
Q61 How important is rehearsing my talk?		☑	☑			☑		77
Q62 Why should I time myself?		☑	☑			☑		79
Q63 How can I limit mistakes?		☑	☑			☑		80
Q64 How important is a dress rehearsal?		☑	☑			☑	☑	81
Q65 Should I trust my equipment?		☑	☑			☑	☑	83
Q66 How can I prepare for questions?			☑			☑		84
Q67 How should I handle questions?			☑					86
Q68 How should I answer questions?			☑					87
Q69 How should I handle difficult or provocative questions?			☑					88
Q70 How should I address tangential questions?			☑	☑				89
Q71 How should I treat a questioner?			☑	☑				90
Q72 Should I always accept a speaking opportunity?						☑		91
Q73 What do I need to know about the length of my talk?						☑		92

PRESENTATION TIPS & TECHNIQUES	Audience	Barriers	Delivery	Feedback	Message	Planning	Props	Page
Q74 Why is awareness of time important?			☑			☑		93
Q75 What are the implications of "when" I speak?						☑		94
Q76 Why should I try to pick my "slot" at a conference?						☑		95
Q77 Why should I find out who else is speaking at a conference?						☑		96
Q78 How can I benefit by listening to other speakers at a conference?			☑			☑		97
Q79 What is essential for an effective team presentation?			☑			☑		98
Q80 What is a key requirement for a team presentation?			☑			☑		99
Q81 What makes a team presentation appear seamless?			☑			☑		100
Q82 Does every presentation need visuals?							☑	101
Q83 What is essential when I design or select visuals?							☑	102
Q84 How do I incorporate visuals effectively?							☑	104
Q85 How can a visual hurt my presentation?							☑	105

PRESENTATION TIPS & TECHNIQUES	Audience	Barriers	Delivery	Feedback	Message	Planning	Props	Page
Q86 How should I use handouts?							☑	106
Q87 How can I ensure my credibility as a speaker?			☑			☑		107
Q88 Which personal attribute is essential to all presentations?			☑					109
Q89 How does attention to detail pay off?			☑			☑		110

ON THE DAY	Audience	Barriers	Delivery	Feedback	Message	Planning	Props	Page
Q90 What should I check prior to speaking?		☑				☑		112
Q91 How should I handle introductions?			☑	☑				114
Q92 How should I handle problems during my presentation?			☑	☑		☑	☑	116
Q93 What can I do if I seem to be losing my audience?	☑		☑					117
Q94 What should I always try to do – hard as it seems?			☑					119

AFTERWARDS	Audience	Barriers	Delivery	Feedback	Message	Planning	Props	Page
Q95 How should I feel when it is done?			☑			☑		120
Q96 What should I reflect on when the presentation is over?			☑			☑		121
Q97 How can I use the questions I was asked to improve my next talk?				☑		☑		122
Q98 What kind of feedback should I seek to help to develop as a speaker?				☑		☑		123
Q99 Can I give the same talk a second, or third, time?	☑					☑		124
Q100 What ongoing activities will help me become an effective speaker?			☑	☑		☑	☑	125

PRESENTATION ESSENTIALS

Q1   What makes an effective speaker?

Think about speakers you have heard throughout your life and in your career. Who are they? You may notice that they have come from all walks of life: politicians, members of the clergy, educators, athletes, entertainers or businesspeople. Can you identify why you recall them? What characteristic brought them to mind? Whatever the specific reason you remember them, *they reached you*.

Good speakers are memorable and have an impact on others. One reason that you remember them is that they recognized their ability to make a difference in their audience's lives. And they used it.

Good speakers respect their audiences and understand how the communication process works. Effective speakers also know what ensures successful communication and what prevents it. They know their own weaknesses as speakers and try to eliminate them. They use their strengths.

They appreciate that the talk they are giving can affect the people to whom they are speaking. They recognize that they can make the audience laugh, take notice, or cry. They also can make an audience angry.

While the topic may or may not always be monumental, the speakers may be suggesting ideas that might make your life easier or more difficult. They may be recommending a new hybrid work policy, the take-over of another company, or the purchase of a particular service or product. While you may not consider introducing a new policy about the lunchroom as earth-shattering, the impact may be a morale booster for the audience thereby indicating to the listeners that the speaker is sensitive to their needs.

Effective speakers recognize the opportunities they have for making change, and they seize the moment. They do not assume that the only important talks that they are going to make are at annual presentations to the Board of Directors or at the Eastern Regional Sales Conference. They know that short in-company talks – whether remote or in person – count, too. For you to be good as a speaker, you should believe that your ideas are important. So, it doesn't matter whether you are speaking to a group of five in an office meeting room or to a group of 400 simultaneously via Zoom in Brussels and New York.

Regardless of the specific subject matter: coffee breaks, remote work, work-life balance, mergers and acquisitions, new product lines, or new passwords to avoid hackers, what you say may have financial or morale or productivity implications for individuals and organizations. Your words have the power to explain, clarify, worry, soothe, encourage, motivate, and / or sell. In effect, when you speak, recognize that the significance of what you are saying has an impact on the people listening to you.

See also

Q5   What are my strengths as a speaker?
Q57   How can I build my confidence as a speaker?
Q60   What kind of set up do I need to ensure a smooth presentation?
Q75   What are the implications of 'when' I speak?
Q96   What should I reflect on when the presentation is over?
Q98   What kind of feedback should I seek to help to develop as a speaker?
Q99   Can I give the same talk a second, or third, time?
Q100   What ongoing activities will help me become an effective speaker?

Q2   What are the steps in the communication process?

Successful athletes, musicians, politicians and businesspeople know their trades. In the same way, to be an effective speaker, you should understand what you are doing when you communicate. Even though it may seem artificial to examine what we take for granted and do every day, it is helpful to consider the individual components in the communication process. While much of the process is instantaneous, by breaking it down into a series of steps you are better able to analyze what you do well or what needs to be improved. In fact, after thinking about the process, you may discover that you have second thoughts about being a spontaneous presenter. Many speakers believe that it is unnecessary to plan or practice, that they can 'shoot from the hip' and still be successful. Usually, they're wrong!

Before we look at each step in more depth, let's examine what we do when we communicate:

- We have a thought or an idea that we will call a "message."
- We want to share that message with an audience.
- We determine the best way to express it.
- We share the message.
- We anticipate feedback.
- We react to the feedback.

Suppose your idea is instituting casual Fridays. You have heard from some colleagues in other organizations that people are more energized at the prospect of wearing less formal clothes once a week. Human resource departments in those organizations have noticed that absenteeism is lower and that people are less stressed and more motivated than the rest of the week. Let's analyze the communication that occurs.

Step one: You believe you have a good idea for your company or your division. At this point, it is simply an idea. It is in your head. But the notion of casual Fridays will be ignored, and never put into practice, unless you share it with others.

Step two: You want to share your idea with the other decision-makers.

Step three: You weigh and decide on the best way to communicate the idea. Emailing? Phoning? Drafting a memo? Instant messaging? Then you consider setting up a virtual meeting. After weighing your options and considering your audience, you decide to include the recommendation in your presentation at the next department meeting.

Step four: You share the idea. You present your recommendation at 2.30pm on Monday via a Zoom meeting.

Step five: You anticipate feedback. You know that some people will reject the notion out of hand – some even may laugh at you – but others may consider it seriously. Someone may thank you for suggesting the idea. You may be challenged to justify your thinking. All of these are reactions to your remarks. They represent feedback.

Step six: You react to that feedback. You take what you were told and learned at the meeting. You combine this with your own views of casual Fridays. You then modify the idea. Based on the feedback, you may decide to make changes, to restate your case or perhaps dismiss the notion because people working from home are casual already. Unless you drop the idea altogether, you will be starting the communication process again with your revised idea. The cycle begins again.

See also

Q3   What can prevent communication?

By considering the communication process as a series of steps, you can determine where breakdowns may occur. Good speakers recognize that even the most effective communication can be blocked. That blockage may occur for many reasons. To eliminate problems, try to control as much of the process as you can. But once you send your message, it is out of your hands. Your idea is in the minds of your receivers. But until then, it is yours to weigh and consider.

Let's look at some of the problems that may occur.

Suppose you have an idea that is unclear. This often happens when ideas have not been thought through sufficiently or what you want to share may be too abstract for the audience.

When you decide to share your idea with someone else, if you have not analyzed your audience well enough, you risk being misunderstood or not understood at all. If you have not anticipated your audience's reactions, your message will not be received – or will be received incorrectly.

Beware of making over generalizations about audiences:

- Avoid making assumptions about the audience's level of knowledge.
- Avoid speaking over their heads.
- Avoid alienating them by speaking down to them.

Audiences are unique because they consist of diverse individuals in varying roles with a wealth of experiences. Thus, they may have differing reactions to what you are saying.

Now suppose you have selected a way to transmit your message. But if you have not selected the best way to send that message, your idea may not be received. Why?

- If you pick the wrong approach, you decrease the chances of your audience understanding what you are saying.
- If you whisper, you may not be heard.

- If you include too many visuals, your images may overwhelm the audience.
- If you use vague words, you may be misinterpreted.
- If you fail to compensate for extraneous noises, you will not be heard.
- If you forget the impact of Zoom, or the time, or the place, you may have an audience that is distracted.

Good speakers recognize that it is easy for a message to be lost or misconstrued. Therefore, they carefully consider their options and make thoughtful choices before they communicate. Consequently, they will be satisfied with what they did after they have spoken.

See also

Q4   How can I identify and eliminate my weaknesses as a speaker?

For you to become a more effective speaker, you should examine your own communication style to determine where or how it may be breaking down. You may ask, "How do I become more aware of my own presentation style?"

You can:

- Take courses in public speaking or in presentation.
- Read books; try *Show Time!*, for instance.
- Ask a colleague for feedback on a presentation.
- Record yourself and listen to the audio / view the video.
- Do all the above.

Look for physical aspects of your presentation that may be problematic to an audience. Consider how you appear. Listen to how you sound. Analyze the organization of your talk. Then think about your talk in terms of your specific audience.

Suppose you identify an aspect of your presentation style that might prevent effective communication. Work at eliminating it. Be realistic. The change won't happen overnight. It takes time. You eliminate any habit, strategy, or technique by catching yourself in the act and trying to change it. But it takes repetition before the change becomes ingrained.

Suppose you are told about a problem, or you spot it yourself when you play back a recording. For example, you discover that you lose the audience because you speak too quickly when you give presentations. To remedy the problem, make a deliberate effort to speak more slowly.

Suppose after watching a recording of yourself, you realize that you confuse the audience because you try to include too much material and your talks are not structured well enough. To remedy the problem, work at organizing your thoughts better.

Avoid berating yourself or becoming overzealous in your determination to reach your goal of excellence as a speaker. Select one area of weakness at a time and work at correcting it. Once you are comfortable with the adjustment, then identify another element that you want to modify and work on that one. Good speakers evolve over time with hard work.

See also

Q5   What are my strengths as a speaker?

Most of us find it easy to criticize ourselves and to identify what we do wrong. In fact, most of us believe that we have many weaknesses. We assume that we are awful speakers, which is why we are so frightened by the prospect of making presentations.

Well, the truth is that you are probably doing any number of things well. Yes, good speakers work at eliminating their weaknesses. But good speakers also recognize their strengths and build on them. Consider some of these attributes:

- You have a clear speech pattern.
- You find it easy to present ideas in a simple form.
- You have a sense of humor.
- You have an easy-going manner.
- You have a pleasant voice.

One or all of them are pluses. Each one can enhance your presentation. When you listen to yourself, when you see yourself played back on a video, or when you ask for a colleague's opinion, be sure to determine exactly what you did that is good. Focus on the positives, rather than the negatives. What you want to do when you are developing as a speaker is to use your strengths at the same time as you are progressively and systematically eliminating the weakness(es) that detract from your work.

See also
Q1   What makes an effective speaker?
Q60   What kind of set up do I need to ensure a smooth presentation?
Q96   What should I reflect on when the presentation is over?
Q98   What kind of feedback should I seek to help to develop as a speaker?
Q100   What ongoing activities will help me become an effective speaker?

Q6   How important is understanding the audience?

An essential part of the communication process is having an idea or thought that you want to share. The notion of sharing is essential to the process. If you forget to unmute yourself in a Zoom meeting, you are unable to share your ideas. If you whisper so that no one in a room can hear you, you are not sharing. To be effective as a speaker, take the time to think about the people with whom you are communicating. Consider your audience.

When you are asked to give a talk or to make a report to a group, it is vital that you get a general impression of the people to whom you will be speaking. A supervisor may say, 'I want you to speak at the annual meeting in February and at the April board meeting.' You may be invited to speak at a management seminar or at a breakfast meeting about marketing strategies. You may be asked to speak about computer applications at a conference.

Too often, however, when we are asked to speak, we focus on the invitation and on the person who extended it. We are flattered, excited or delighted. Our egos are fed by the recognition. We are thrilled and then terrified at the prospect. If this reaction is true for you, rein in your conflicting emotions and remember to ask questions about your audience to get an overview of who will be present. Ask why the meeting is being held. Find out how many people will attend and ask about their general areas of expertise. Add some invaluable hard data to enable you to make educated choices

See also
Q7   What do I need to know about the audience?
Q8   Who should I address my talk to?
Q9   Why is the audience attending my talk?
Q10   How can I benefit from analyzing the relationships among the audience members?

Q7   What do I need to know about the audience?

An overview of the audience is important as are the details.

Suppose you have been asked to speak to the board or to a group at a conference. You have determined how many will be present. You also know the purpose of the meeting. But you have other questions to ask. While they may not suit every situation, some of them might include:

- What are the job titles of the people in the audience?
- What is their native language? Does everyone speak English?
- Where are they from? What country? What region?
- What are their ages?
- What are their genders?
- What do they know about the subject?
- What is their training?
- Why are they attending?
- Who else will be speaking?
- What are the topics of any other speakers?

It takes only a few minutes to ask the organizer questions like these. Do ask them. The more you know about the audience, the more you can tailor what you are going to say to them, thus increasing the odds that you will be understood. And you will avoid mis-communication.

The answers to your questions may help you decide about the amount of explaining you will have to do, the types of visuals you might use, or the approach you might take. For example, analogies to American football may not work well with a group of French executives. References to crowded buses, trains and airports may be inappropriate for a talk in a rural area. Nor will the agonies of snow shoveling be readily understood in mild climates. In the same way, a group of marketing managers may require more background on the financials of a recommendation than those trained in accountancy.

Get details; know your audience.

See also

Q6   How important is understanding the audience?
Q8   Who should I address my talk to?
Q9   Why is the audience attending my talk?
Q10 How can I benefit from analyzing the relationships among the
         audience members?

Q8   Who should I address my talk to?

To know your audience, try to get as many names and job titles as you can. The more you know about the people who will be listening to you the better you can adapt your subject to their expertise.

Once you know who is attending, be careful. Many speakers make unwise assumptions. They learn that the CEO or divisional manager will be in attendance. Because they consider the position critical to the decision-making process, such speakers decide to pitch the entire talk to that one person. That is an unwise decision for two reasons:

- First, you can alienate other people in the room if you discount them and direct your thoughts only to the most senior person present.

- Second, you are making assumptions about who has influence over whom or whose opinions are sought out or valued by that senior manager. Frequently, senior people ask the opinions of their assistants. Remember, even Don Corleone had a *consigliere*. You may not know who that person (or people) may be.

Therefore, address everyone present – whether management or support staff. Value everyone. Prepare your thoughts with the entire audience in mind.

See also
Q6   How important is understanding the audience?
Q7   What do I need to know about the audience?
Q9   Why is the audience attending my talk?
Q10   How can I benefit from analyzing the relationships among the audience members?

Q9   Why is the audience attending my talk?

Based on who is going to be present, discover, if you can, why they will be attending. In many instances, the audience's level of interest will affect their reactions to what you are saying. For example, find out whether:

- People *want* to be there or have been *ordered* to be.
- People were sent to the meeting because someone else was unavailable.
- Someone thought that attending would be important for a specific person's development or position.

If you are speaking at a conference, consider how many people are attending the meeting because it is an opportunity to spend a weekend in Paris or because they genuinely value the issues being addressed by those who are speaking. In essence, the motivation of the people in front of you affects your planning.

See also
Q6   How important is understanding the audience?
Q7   What do I need to know about the audience?
Q8   Who should I address my talk to?
Q10   How can I benefit from analyzing the relationships among the audience members?

Q10   How can I benefit from analyzing the relationships among the audience members?

People have influence over each other. Neither overestimate nor underestimate that fact when you are talking to a group. While some people take only their own counsel, most of us weigh the opinions of others before making final decisions.

Some members of your audience may have their own personal political agendas. They may want to demonstrate their intellect or their ability to confront or argue, not so much to challenge your ideas but to demonstrate their skills in front of the others in the room. In other words, questions from some people may derive more from their own needs than from the issues that you are raising in your presentation.

Some people may be resentful of others because they were ordered to attend the meeting. Other people may be feeling proud because they were told that they would benefit from attending.

Therefore, consider the individuals in your audience and consider their relationships to and with each other:

- Are they genuinely interested in your subject?
- Are people present who are seeking to advance their careers?
- Have some others been denied recent promotions?
- Are some people waiting for contract agreements to be settled?
- Are some people feeling that they know more than others because they have worked for the company longer and yet are unable to advance because they lack the appropriate credentials?
- Are some people jealous of your opportunity to speak?

When members of the audience ask you questions, you should think about where those questions are coming from. Think about what is motivating your questioners and who they may be trying to impress. Consider the implication of different jobs and titles on attitudes toward your topic. Consider differing perspectives.

The more you take the make-up of your audience into your planning, the more effective your talk will be.

See also
Q6   How important is understanding the audience?
Q7   What do I need to know about the audience?
Q8   Who should I address my talk to?
Q9   Why is the audience attending my talk?

Q11   What is the message of my talk?

You can analyze your audience, respect their abilities and diversity and admire their talent but you cannot control their reactions. However, you can control the content of the talk. Advising you to 'have a message' may sound basic. Be sure you do.

When we were children, we may have been told, "Don't say anything unless you have something to say." What does it mean? It means that you should have ideas that are important enough to share. When you think about the talks that you have heard throughout your life, you will remember some good ones and some poor ones. Perhaps one of the basic problems with the poor talks was that the speech suffered because the message was unclear to the speaker. Under those circumstances, how could it make sense to the audience?

To be a good speaker, you should know *exactly* what you want to talk about, not just "sort of" know. Let's suppose that you plan to evaluate levels of productivity, or to give a monthly departmental progress report or to discuss an adjustment in the budget. You know you have to say something about productivity, progress or the budget. While that's a good start for your planning, you need more to formulate your message.

You should know *exactly* what that "something" is. And that something is often called the "hook." You look for a way to make your message important to your listeners – and then you literally "reel them in."

See also
Q2   What are the steps in the communication process?
Q12   What is the purpose of my talk?
Q13   How can I anticipate objections to my message?
Q14   What should I eliminate as I prepare my presentation?
Q20   How should I organize the body of my talk?

Q12   What is the purpose of my talk?

A good speaker assumes the responsibility for both knowing the message and explaining its purpose.

You may say, "Of course, I know my purpose. I am going to talk about productivity, progress, or the budget." Yes, but let's step back for a moment. Let's use the example of casual Fridays: suppose that's your message. To be effective, you should be able to articulate what they are and *why* you are talking about them.

In the same way, you should be able to say why you are talking about productivity and how you intend to influence the audience's thinking about the subject. What is it about the budget that is important for this audience to understand? Are you overspending? Is there a surplus in some area? Do you need to anticipate a major expenditure?

Having a purpose means knowing what you want the audience to do or say or think as a result of what you are telling them. It isn't enough to say, "I'm talking about casual Fridays." You should be able to articulate to yourself and to the audience why what you are saying matters. You want your listeners to consider your subject for a reason. If you cannot articulate why the audience will benefit from hearing your progress report, you will be less successful as a speaker. Audiences are more attentive when they believe that the subject is relevant to them.

See also
Q11   What is the message of my talk?
Q13   How can I anticipate objections to my message?
Q20   How should I organize the body of my talk?

Q13   How can I anticipate objections to my message?

To anticipate objections, you should consider your knowledge of the audience. To anticipate challenges, think about who will be listening to you. The more you know about the makeup of your group, the better able you will be to put yourself into their shoes. Only then can you try to think from their unique perspectives.

Your knowledge of the audience's personalities, responsibilities, and attitudes helps you determine which elements of your talk might be challenged or which of your ideas might be dismissed as being frivolous.

Suppose your talk focuses on the importance of providing better technology for people working remotely. The company has already spent vast sums on technology upgrades, but you know that many people are struggling with their old computers. Be sensitive to their level of knowledge and budgetary concerns. Otherwise, your talk may fall on deaf ears.

In the same way, a talk to members of a creative department might be different from a talk to a group of financial planners, while a talk to management might be different from one given to a group in editorial.

When you prepare your talk, think about what arguments might arise based on the perspectives of your audience. Build your responses right into the talk. If you can anticipate the creative department's concerns, then you can indicate to them your awareness by saying, "Some of you may not agree that that these upgrades will allow you to ... but they can, because ..." When you fail to anticipate certain fundamental arguments, you may find that your audience resists your ideas from the outset. You can free them to listen by overcoming their objections.

Q14   What should I eliminate as I prepare my presentation?

Often, talks are too general. Frequently, they are loaded with unnecessary verbiage. Remember that your objective is to get your message across to your audience. Your message is what you want people to do or to understand as a result of what you say. Therefore, if you clutter your talk with tangential data, interesting anecdotes about trips you have taken or endless implementation strategies, more than likely little of your actual message will be understood, recalled or acted upon.

The phrase "Keep it simple, stupid" is true for speeches. As you review your talk, check that everything that you are including relates directly to what you are trying to convince the audience to do. Even if your talk is intended to introduce another speaker at a meeting or to provide an entertaining chat at a dinner, stay on your topic. If you are asked to praise Caesar, praise Caesar rather than spending valuable time talking about how nervous you are — unless of course, Caesar has been helping you to overcome your nervousness.

You may be attached to some of your stories, analogies or data. Remember, good stories are good stories. You can always use your data or your anecdotes in other speeches where they are more appropriate.

So, eliminate everything from your presentation that undermines your aim of communicating your message to your audience.

See also
Q2   What are the steps in the communication process?
Q11   What is the message of my talk?
Q12   What is the purpose of my talk?

Q15 What approach to the subject should I choose?

Suppose you know *what* you are going to say, and you know *why* you are saying it. You also have thought about the nature of your audience. Therefore, you realize where in the talk you might have to clarify or support your ideas because of differing viewpoints. You have accomplished a great deal.

Now you choose your approach. A formal 20-minute talk may be inappropriate for an in-person breakfast meeting or a lunch at a nearby pub. Think about the situation and the setting. So instead of talking for the entire time, you may decide to talk for five minutes and answer questions for 15. A 20-minute talk on a complex subject may require you to use more visuals than for a talk that is less complicated. Given the subject or the time available for speaking, you may want to keep the talk light-hearted and casual, or you may want it to be earnest and serious.

Consider:

- Perhaps you want to talk at the audience the whole time.
- Perhaps you want to involve them not only by having them ask questions, but also by having them do something.
- Perhaps you want breakout sessions after you have spoken.
- Perhaps you want to raise questions and allow people to talk to their neighbors before answering you.

In other words, depending upon the situation, the topic, your purpose and your audience, select an approach that will best accomplish your goal, which remains the same – getting your message across.

See also

DEVELOPING A PRESENTATION

Q16   How important is the audience's first impression of a speaker?

Most of us make judgements about other people within seconds of seeing or meeting them. Right or wrong, as members of the audience, we look at speakers before their talks and make decisions about them. We look at the height, shape, age, sex, or ethnicity of the person who is going to speak and make a judgement. We look at the way speakers move or dress, and we evaluate them. We look at how organized they are with their notes or handouts or how comfortable they appear to be with the technology they are using. All of this happens before the speaker has even said a word.

With that in mind, it is important for you to put your best foot forward before you begin. So, when you do begin to speak, your opening movements and words need to be well-chosen. The beginning of your talk is not the time for you to be adjusting your clothing, fiddling with papers, or apologizing for being late. This is not the time to straighten a tie or tap on the microphone. What you do first is what the audience remembers.

Therefore, the beginning of your talk is the time to look at the audience confidently, smile and utter a well-prepared opening sentence.

See also

Q1   What makes an effective speaker?
Q17   What motivational techniques can I use to grab the audience's attention?
Q18   Why is it important to state my purpose?
Q19   What value is there in explaining my format?
Q38   Why is eye contact key to effective presenting?
Q44   What should I consider when selecting what I wear?
Q45   What should I consider when selecting my shoes?
Q46   What should I consider about the way I wear my hair?

Q17   What motivational techniques can I use to grab the audience's attention?

Your listeners lead busy lives: they have families, cars, jobs, bills to pay, reports to write and groceries to buy. So, your job as a speaker is to stop everyone from thinking about their other responsibilities and to focus on what you have to say. In essence, grab the audience's attention.

There are tried and tested techniques you may want to consider using:

- Open with a quotation.
- Ask a question.
- Tell a relevant story or anecdote.
- Make a provocative statement.
- Use a shocking statistic.
- Show a well-designed visual.

In other words, assume that the audience is still focused on what they were doing before they sat down or came into the room. That's where their minds are. They are preoccupied with what they just heard, with conversations they were having, with their personal lives, with the lunches they didn't care for, coffee they meant to get, or a report they must finish. You, as speaker, have the job of distracting them from their own thoughts and giving them a reason to be more interested in your ideas than in their current ones. Your well-chosen opening words and actions do just that.

See also
Q16   How important is the audience's first impression of a speaker?
Q43   Can my movements motivate the audience?
Q48   How does altering the volume of my voice motivate the audience?
Q52   Why is enthusiasm essential?

Q18   Why is it important to state my purpose?

It is important that your opening words have the effect of getting your audience's attention and taking them away from their own concerns or pressures. But you cannot stop there:

- Hold their attention by clearly stating your purpose.
- Tell them why your subject matter has an impact on them.
- Give them a reason for needing your information.
- Connect your subject matter to their jobs or responsibilities.

In essence, make your ideas relevant.

How often have you heard talks and were unsure what the speaker was talking about and what it had to do with you? Speakers frequently fail to state explicitly the purpose of the talk. You should.

If you have made a strong opening sentence, told a story or a joke, then you explain how that sentence, story or joke relates to the message. State your purpose. Do not assume that your listeners know your intent just because they received a memo inviting them to the meeting or a program with the title of your talk printed on it.

Consider saying something like, "We are here to discuss the implications of budget cuts on the company restaurant," or "This morning we will examine the proposed changes in the accounting system and its impact on your department." That statement clarifies your purpose for your audience. They now know what you plan to do, or at least part of it.

See also

Q19   What value is there in explaining my format?

You have given the audience a reason to listen, and you have their attention. You have told them what you are going to discuss. Then tell them what approach you are using to explain your view or to support your position. You are giving them a road map and telling them how you are going to get them there and how long it is going to take.

You might say, "In the next 20 minutes, we will discuss four aspects of our investigation into our current appraisal system. First, we will examine the problems we have experienced with the system. Second, we will explain how we analyzed those problems. Third, we will present our conclusions and, fourth, we will make two recommendations to simplify the process and to eliminate the issues we have identified to ensure that the system is more effective in future."

In other words, tell the audience exactly what you are going to do. Remember that, for the most part, you are asking people to retain information by depending on their ability to listen (and research shows that people retain less than 10% of what they hear). The road map that you give them will help them anticipate where you are going and how long it will take.

Remember what you asked your parents or what your little ones ask you: "Are we there yet?" To avoid that question (which frequently indicates boredom), as a speaker, tell your audience where you are going, how long it will take, and the route.

See also
Q15   What approach to the subject should I choose?
Q18   Why is it important to state my purpose?
Q20   How should I organize the body of my talk?

Q20   How should I organize the body of my talk?

The beginning of your talk is when you grab the audience's attention, present your message, and explain your purpose and approach. The middle section provides you with the opportunity to present your ideas in an orderly fashion. To help your listeners stay focused and retain information, provide them with a structure.

When you are putting your thoughts together or looking through your material in preparation for your talk, try to find a natural order. Ask yourself:

- Can I break down the topic into two parts, such as causes and effects or advantages and disadvantages?

- Can I organize the material from an historical perspective? Can I plan to discuss what used to be, what currently is and what will be?

- Can I use a SWOT analysis? Can I discuss strengths, weaknesses, opportunities, and threats?

- Can I present my research by asking a question, showing the methodology for answering the question, explaining the findings, and making the recommendations?

There is no one way or perfect model to use every time you speak. The nature of your topic will determine the structure. But it is always helpful to you and to your audience if you select a clear one.

The process of organizing your thoughts is the same approach you would use if you were writing a report. You look for some natural order that enables your readers to follow your logic. The same is true for listeners.

Remember though, with a report, readers always can return to a previous paragraph or section if they get lost. Listeners cannot. If you are unstructured, and the audience gets lost, they may not be able to find you again. In fact, they may not *want* to.

See also
Q2   What are the steps in the communication process?
Q18   Why is it important to state my purpose?
Q19   What value is there in explaining my format?
Q21   Is using numbers a useful organizing structure?
Q22   Is using chronology a useful organizing structure?
Q23   Is order of importance a useful organizing structure?
Q24   Are mnemonics a useful organizing structure?

Q21   Is using numbers a useful organizing structure?

You have decided on a basic structure for your talk, such as cause and effect, before and after, advantages or disadvantages, or conclusions and recommendations. Now think about how you can create internal order within one or more of those sections.

One way to organize is by using numbers. "This morning we are examining five methods for ensuring that we eliminate our problems with the new phone system." Begin by saying "First," then discuss point one. Follow this by saying "Second" and then discuss point two and so on. When you tell your audience to expect five items, they will expect five. Remember to go over five, not four or seven. You promised.

If you do decide to use numbers, be sure to say the number before you make the next point. "The third reason we are working during the holiday period is ... "

And when you announce how many items to expect, repeat each number before you start that section. People should remember your reasoning.

See also
Q20   How should I organize the body of my talk?
Q22   Is using chronology a useful organizing structure?
Q23   Is order of importance a useful organizing structure?
Q25   Is it wrong to repeat information?
Q26   When is it useful to locate information by clarifying spatial relations?

Q22 Is using chronology a useful organizing structure?

Another method of helping your audience retain information is to structure your thoughts chronologically. What you do is discuss what happened in the past, continue into the present and then forecast the future. You can also use reverse chronology if you wish. Either way, you have a plan.

If you are describing an event such as an accident that occurred in a short period of time, do the same thing: what happened first, then 10 minutes later, then 15 minutes after that.

Only you can make the decision about whether chronology works for you. The nature of your subject may dictate if it will or won't.

Remember, too, depending on the age or knowledge of your audience, if you use chronology, you may need to provide an historical context. You may need to begin by saying: "Not all of you were here three years ago when we instituted the flexi-time scheduling. Therefore, let's begin by looking at what we were experiencing when we introduced it."

See also
Q20 How should I organize the body of my talk?
Q21 Is using numbers a useful organizing structure?
Q23 Is order of importance a useful organizing structure?
Q24 Are mnemonics a useful organizing structure?
Q25 Is it wrong to repeat information?
Q26 When is it useful to locate information by clarifying spatial relations?

Q23   Is order of importance a useful organizing structure?

When you structure your thoughts, you may decide that some of your ideas or recommendations are weightier than others. You believe that the audience will value some of your ideas more than others. You may want to put your recommendations in order of importance. Remember that most of us retain the first and last items in a series better than the items in the middle.

So, you may want to put your most critical point first and then your other points in a descending order of importance. You may want to reverse it. Or you may want to have an important point first, a relatively weak one in the middle and the strongest at the end. You are deciding that you want the audience to remember what you said just before you left the meeting.

Again, it doesn't matter which order you select. What matters is that you have a sequence.

Bear in mind, regardless of the sequence — strongest argument first or last — be consistent whenever you repeat the same items. Stay in the same order in the beginning, in the middle and at the end of your talk.

See also
Q20   How should I organize the body of my talk?
Q21   Is using numbers a useful organizing structure?
Q22   Is using chronology a useful organizing structure?
Q24   Are mnemonics a useful organizing structure?
Q25   Is it wrong to repeat information?
Q26   When is it useful to locate information by clarifying spatial relations?

Q24 Are mnemonics a useful organizing structure?

Another way of aiding memory is by using mnemonics. These are devices designed to help us recall information. Some of us create them in our everyday lives. Perhaps a password or pin you created is a mnemonic.

Suppose your mnemonic is the list of chores that you have when you leave the office – DEAL – to remind you to pick up the **D**og from the vet, buy some **E**ggs in the supermarket, get cash at the **A**TM and collect the **L**awnmower from the repair shop. Sounds silly, but we all create ways of keeping information in our heads. Given how hectic life is, sometimes a word or phrase will do.

The same technique for aiding memory may be useful for some talks. If you see that you can create a memorable word or phrase from the first letter of the key words or ideas in your arguments, then do so. The audience is more likely to remember your argument – but be sure that they remember what the letters represent rather than your mnemonic.

See also

Q20 How should I organize the body of my talk?
Q21 Is using numbers a useful organizing structure?
Q22 Is using chronology a useful organizing structure?
Q23 Is order of importance a useful organizing structure?
Q25 Is it wrong to repeat information?
Q26 When is it useful to locate information by clarifying spatial relations?

Q25   Is it wrong to repeat information?

Speaking of repetition, let's emphasize the importance of repeating. Remember that people are depending primarily on their ears for absorbing what you are saying. Therefore, it is important to repeat. Repeat. Repeat and repeat. In fact, if you make a point in the opening, nothing prevents you from saying it again in the middle of the talk. And say it again in the last section.

Suppose your position is that virtual parties will make a difference for morale. Say it several times. What you want is for people to leave remembering those words. Advertisers do it. Politicians do it. Repeat the words or sentences you want people to hold on to.

Repetition is important if you are using numbers, too. "We have considered the first reason, cost. Now let's look at the second, quality." Then, in the conclusion, you speak again of the two reasons: cost and quality.

Repetition is essential when you are relying primarily on an audience's ears. Unless you record your thoughts or post them online, or distribute a hard copy at the door , what you said is all they have. And they will have heard it only once. All the more reason to repeat at the end what you said at the outset or what has been a theme throughout. "Therefore, in conclusion, we recommend that ..." Say it again.

See also
Q2   What are the steps in the communication process?
Q14   What should I eliminate as I prepare my presentation?
Q27   How can I conclude a talk effectively?

Q26   When is it useful to locate information by clarifying spatial relations?

Much of what we talk about nowadays in a global economy involves location or geography. If you are talking about your global network, your new office lay-out, your new offices or even your new logo, it is helpful to make a conscious effort to work from top to bottom, from bottom to top, from left to right or from right to left.

If you are describing the plan for your new offices, take the audience from the entrance to the rear, or move them around the offices in a clockwise or counter-clockwise direction. It is easier to visualize or retain information if you are talking about doing business in different counties or countries, moving in a specific direction – east to west, west to east, north to south and so on.

See also
Q20   How should I organize the body of my talk?
Q21   Is using numbers a useful organizing structure?
Q22   Is using chronology a useful organizing structure?
Q23   Is order of importance a useful organizing structure?

Q27   How can I conclude a talk effectively?

The beginning of a talk is the opportunity to get your audience's attention. The middle permits you to develop your ideas. The final part allows you to restate your ideas or present conclusions or recommendations clearly and emphatically.

Your entire talk is a package. It should sound as if it has been put together, wrapped and tied up neatly. You do that, in part, by having the end mirror the beginning. When you decide how you are going to structure your talk and how you are going to begin it, be sure that your ending is consistent with that opening:

- If you began with a joke, conclude with a similar related joke.
- If you began with a quotation, end with another or the same quotation.
- If you began with a mnemonic, repeat it at the end.
- If you began with a question, ask another one or repeat your original question and answer it.
- If you began with a shocking statistic, end with another sort of statistic or indicate that your recommendations will alter that statistic.

In other words, make sure that the ending is consistent with and reinforces what you have said in your opening remarks. "That is why I began by saying ..."

And when you say that you are concluding, please conclude. The number of speakers who say that they are about to finish and then continue for several more minutes is amazing. Some speakers say, "In conclusion ...," followed shortly thereafter by "Finally ...," and then "One last point before I leave you ..." Once you signal that you are concluding by saying words that indicate an ending, end.

See also
Q16   How important is the audience's first impression of a speaker?

Q17   What motivational techniques can I use to grab the audience's
attention?
Q27   How can I conclude a talk effectively?
Q28   How should I handle courtesies like "thank you"?

Q28   How should I handle courtesies like "thank you"?

Remember your closing remarks are critical for your listeners. End with a strong statement and with a strong image.

Avoid having your last words be some sort of apology like, "I hope I haven't taken up too much of your time," or "I am sorry that we ran a few minutes late," or "Thank you for listening." Such comments may seem charming, self-effacing or polite, but these words distract from your final, powerful words about your message. What the audience hears last is your apology rather than hearing your view of the issues.

Make your final statement. Take a deep breath. Wait. Look around. If you feel you should do so, say one brief "Thank you." It is enough.

Then, unless you are taking questions from the floor, take your seat. Don't drop your shoulders, mop your brow, cast your eyes to the heavens, or let out a sigh of relief. Maintain a strong, memorable, positive image.

See also
Q27   How can I conclude a talk effectively?
Q67   How should I handle questions?
Q91   How should I handle introductions?

PRESENTATION TIPS & TECHNIQUES

Q29   Should I avoid jargon and colloquialisms?

Having a worthwhile idea is essential to giving a powerful talk. But it takes more than a good idea to create an excellent speech. Structuring your talk is important as are your word choices.

Time and again, you have heard the phrase "Avoid jargon." But it is easy to fall into using it, especially if you work with people who write or speak it in the office. It's remarkable how words like "transparent" or "synergistic" become commonplace in a short time. Some people seem to think that it is mundane to "talk" or "meet." Apparently "interfacing" or "liaising" with a member of a committee is an executive privilege while talking is not. "Meet" and "talk" are perfectly good words and are readily understood by most of us, so use them.

If you want to keep your message clear and easily understood, keep it simple and avoid "ninjas," "low-hanging fruit," "inputs," "outputs" and "throughputs."

Bear in mind that your audience may include people from different parts of the country, of the continent, or of the world. So:

- A phrase you grew up using in the North may not be understood in the South.
- What you say in the city may not be commonly understood by someone from the country.
- An expression you learned from your parents may no longer be in use by a member of a younger generation.

Listen to teenagers for a few minutes. You will hear words that their peer group or social media has introduced into the language that you may not understand. So, when you review your talk, be sure that the phrases you are using are familiar to all your listeners.

See also
Q30   Should I explain technical language?
Q31   Am I aware of my verbal idiosyncrasies?

Q30   Should I explain technical language?

Many of us use the technical language of our career specializations as if the vocabulary were common to everyone. Doctors do it. Lawyers do it. Computer analysts do it. Marketing executives do it. Hoteliers do it. Every field has its own unique vocabulary. So be sure that your audience is familiar with the terminology. If you know that the audience is not, then take a moment to define technical terms.

How do you know if they are familiar with the words? Audience analysis will help you determine whether you will have to explain your word choices. If you are speaking about a new computer application and everyone in the room is familiar with it, there is no need to explain. But if only 10 per cent of your audience are using it, you may have to take time to explain what you mean.

How do you explain? You can give your explanations as you go , or you can provide a handout with significant terms to which you refer – or use visuals. And remember acronyms and abbreviations should be explained as well.

You may argue that you don't have enough time for definitions. But, if your audience is unable to comprehend what you mean, then whatever time you save is irrelevant because they are unable to decode your message.

See also
Q29   Should I avoid jargon and colloquialisms?
Q31   Am I aware of my verbal idiosyncrasies?

Q31   Am I aware of my verbal idiosyncrasies?

Your word choices may come from your upbringing, your education, or perhaps from your career specialization. Some words may come from habit. For example:

- Do you say, "You know" or "Right?" frequently when you are speaking?
- Do you say "like" at the end of sentences?
- Do you have a pet word like "absolutely" or "marvelous" that you sprinkle around unnecessarily?

Whatever the word, try to notice it. Think whether you have any pet phrases. Catch yourself using them and try to eliminate them over time. Don't berate yourself if you hear yourself using "irregardless" for the third time. Just decrease the number of repetitions.

What you are trying to avoid is having your audience distracted by focusing on your pet phrase. What you want is for them to remember your message. Since repetition increases the odds of someone retaining your words; sometimes you don't want certain phrases retained.

See also
Q3   What can prevent communication?
Q29   Should I avoid jargon and colloquialisms?
Q30   Should I explain technical language?

Q32 Should I read my paper?

Some people feel that a speaker looks more professional if they speak off-the-cuff. Think twice before you make the decision to avoid notes and to be a spontaneous speaker – it's more challenging than it appears. But, whatever you do, please avoid reading to your audience.

True, there are times that you must "deliver a paper" the way academics do. For the most part, though, the process is deadly dull for the audience. The truth is that they could read your paper at their leisure, possibly get more out of it, and be in more comfortable surroundings. If the audience knows that they can get a copy (or they already have a copy) of what you are reading to them, they may not even listen to what you are saying when you are at the podium. The value of speaking instead of reading is that it allows you to react to what is happening around you.

There is another reason to avoid reading. When you read, of necessity your eyes are focused on the paper in front of you – unless you have a teleprompter. While you are reading, you cannot see what is going on in the audience. You cannot see whether people are looking confused or tired, or whether someone has a question. Eye-contact is essential for a good talk. Reading prevents that.

Furthermore, when you read, you tilt your head down and your voice is projected down as well. Unless you have a mic, your audience has more difficulty hearing you --another good reason to avoid reading your paper.

See also
Q17   What motivational techniques can I use to grab the audience's attention?
Q33   Should I use notes?
Q86   How should I use handouts?

Q33   Should I use notes?

Yes, you should have notes of some kind. If you choose cards, they give you something to do with your hands. To be clear, notes serve two basic purposes:

- First, they help you from forgetting what you have planned to say. It can happen. People panic. Some folks are so terrified in the opening minutes that they go blank. They remember nothing. I know: I have been there. Having notes means you have something to fall back on should you suffer from such a violent attack of nerves that you are unable to continue.

- Second, notes are invaluable if you talk too much – instead of too little. Some speakers enjoy the sense of power over their audience; others are natural storytellers or go off on tangents. They spontaneously recollect additional anecdotes or delight in interrupting their own presentations by providing lengthy answers to unasked questions. They easily talk for 30 minutes longer than scheduled. Notes rein them in. Notes remind you of your original plans and assist you by helping you return to them. No matter how enthralling your talk may be, audiences have other obligations.

See also
Q17   What motivational techniques can I use to grab the audience's attention?
Q32   Should I read my paper?
Q62   Why should I time myself?
Q74   Why is awareness of time important?
Q86   How should I use handouts?

Q34 What kind of notes should I use?

Some people use their laptops with notes for their presentation; others use a sheet of paper with key points; some use their phones. I prefer to use cards which fit in a pocket, handbag or briefcase.

When you use cards, you are free of a lectern on which to rest papers or your laptop They allow you to keep your head up because you can bring your cards up rather than look down. You need only look down to check and then look up to speak. Thus, you can keep your eyes on the audience. With your head up, you can project your voice better. In an in-person event, you are free to walk to the back of the room. If you use your phone, explain that your notes are on it. It may look as if you are checking texts. Phones also narrow your focus.

Cards allow you to practice anywhere with ease and flexibility. You can take them out on the plane, the train, your office, or at home.

What should you put on the cards?
They are cue cards. They are prompts. Number each card consecutively – it is easy for them to get mixed up. Use only one side, put one or two of your main ideas. Write a key word or phrase like "red car" or "John's report" to remind you of the material you are going to use to support your argument.

No need to write it all out word-for-word except, if you anticipate being nervous, then you may want to write out the first few sentences, or the names of significant people who need to be identified or thanked.

How many cards should you have?
There is no rule. You may have as few as five cards, or as many as 50. Be patient with yourself. If you have never used cards before, they take some adjustment. But once you get the feel of looking down, checking and then looking up to continue, you will discover that they give you security and freedom.

See also

Q32   Should I read my paper?

Q33   Should I use notes?

Q61   How important is rehearsing my talk?

Q35   Is it better to stand still or move around?

If you are using cards, you can use the space around you. You can move. You can walk around. During a 10- or 15- minute talk or even a longer one, a speaker who moves around is more motivating to listeners and is easier to pay attention to than a static figure – a key problem with virtual meetings. When you move closer to individuals or to sections of your audience, those individuals or groups become more attentive.

"Reading a paper" or having your notes on your laptop may keep you glued to one spot because you need a table or a lectern. If it is a lectern, the audience can only see your shoulders and your head, not your entire body. You may be unable to move much to the right or to the left. Your use of your hands is limited, because they may be turning pages. Unless you are very tall or have an adjustable stand on which to place your papers, you may be lost behind the box. Basically, the more fixed you are in one spot, the less interesting you are to your audience. The less interesting you are, the harder it is for the audience to concentrate for a long period on what you are saying.

See also

Q17   What motivational techniques can I use to grab the audience's attention?

Q37   How can I use my head effectively?

Q42   What does the audience notice about the way I move my feet?

Q43   Can my movements motivate the audience?

Q36   Why should I pay attention to my posture?

As a child, you were probably told to "stand up straight and don't slouch." Well, you are about to hear it again. Standing up straight allows you to breathe more deeply, which is calming, and to project your voice more effectively. Another reason for standing tall is that you appear more confident.

Can you visualize speakers you have heard in the past?

- Some stand with one hip up and one shoulder down looking very much like a cowboy who has just ridden into town.

- Other speakers shift their weight back and forth from one leg to the other.

- Still others lean on the lectern or table in front of them or rock back and forth.

- Others rock up and back on their toes.

These movements detract from what you are saying because they, rather than your words, become the focus of the audience's attention.

Ideally, when you are standing still, have your legs far enough apart to support your weight. Imagine drawing a line from your shoulders straight down; where the line touches the floor is where your feet should be -- about eight to 10 inches apart – more if you are tall. If you stand with your feet touching each other, you may find yourself rocking from side to side as if you were a tree being blown by a high wind. Posture matters.

See also
Q16   How important is the audience's first impression of a speaker?
Q35   Is it better to stand still or move around?
Q37   How can I use my head effectively?
Q40   What should I do with my arms and hands?
Q41   Why should I become aware of and avoid distracting gestures?

Q37 How can I use my head effectively?

Of course, you say, "use your head" if you are going to give a talk. But, literally, *use* your head. Hold it up and lift your chin – but no so high you risk looking arrogant. Look out toward your audience.

Your head can be expressive and should be consistent with your words. There is no reason why you cannot shake your head "No" if you are saying something negative; nod your head slightly when your remarks are positive. If you are making a quizzical remark, you can tilt it to the side.

This recommendation is not suggesting you plan and rehearse your head movements. Simply use your head naturally, in the same way you would if you were engaged in a conversation. In that situation, you would agree, disagree, think, appear pleased or bewildered simply by moving your head. Do the same when you speak to an audience of more than one.

See also
Q36 Why should I pay attention to my posture?
Q40 What should I do with my arms and hands?
Q41 Why should I become aware of and avoid distracting gestures?
Q42 What does the audience notice about the way I move my feet?

Q38   Why is eye contact key to effective presenting?

The eyes have been called the "windows of the soul." They are also the keys to giving effective presentations. No matter how hard it may be for you to look at the faces of your audience, look at them. Really look at them. See them. The only times you should take your eyes off them is when you are checking your notes, or addressing a technical issue.

Look at the audience – at everybody. In person, move your eyes around the room. Look at those in the back. Look at the people in the front. Look at the people on the sides. Please refrain from talking to a window or over the heads of the audience. Virtually look at the camera, and talk to your audience.

The reason that you are looking at the audience is to show them that you are earnest about what you are saying. In addition, you are looking at them to see whether and how they are reacting to what you are telling them. Being aware of that second aspect is critical. See how the audience is responding to what you are saying so that you can alter, emphasize, clarify or reinforce your point(s). For example:

- If they are falling asleep, you may have to find a way to wake them up.
- If they look confused, you may have to repeat or clarify, or anticipate a question.
- If they look angry, you may have to anticipate some questions.

In other words, look at your audience, let them see your face and react to what you see them doing as you speak.

One *caveat*: be careful of focusing on a friend, a power figure or a "nodder." In your desire to please, it is easy to direct your talk toward one person rather than the whole group. Catch yourself and look around the entire room. In person, if most people are sitting in one section, look at any area where only a few people are seated.

See also
Q37 How can I use my head effectively?
Q39 Is it wrong to smile when presenting?

Q39   Is it wrong to smile when presenting?

Being advised to look pleasant may seem silly to you. But once again, recall speakers you have heard. Many people have sour or sullen faces at the beginning of a talk and continue to look that way until the end. If you want your audience to react positively to what you are saying, your face, like your head, should mirror your words. If you are proud or enthusiastic about your message, then your face should look proud and enthusiastic. If you are concerned, look concerned. If you are amused, look amused. If you are startled, look startled.

Do smile. Some people think that presenting is such a serious business that you must look earnest. Smiling does not detract from the seriousness of your message.

Of course, you should be sensible. Smiles are inappropriate when you are announcing lay-offs, budget freezes or other bad news, unless your motive is to be cynical and sinister. But do smile when what you are saying is upbeat and has positive implications for the people in front of you. The audience will like you more and pay more attention to your message.

See also

Q11   What is the message of my talk?
Q38   Why is eye contact key to effective presenting?
Q41   Why should I become aware of and avoid distracting gestures?
Q50   Should I change my personality when I speak?
Q52   Why is enthusiasm essential?
Q54   How can I handle my own nervous reactions?
Q88   Which personal attribute is essential to all presentations?

Q40   What should I do with my arms and hands?

Your arms and hands are both the most valuable and least expensive visuals that you have. Take advantage of them.

When you give a talk:

- Avoid putting one or both hands in your pockets.
- Avoid putting your hand in your pocket and playing with your keys or your loose change.
- Avoid putting your hands behind your back.
- Avoid fidgeting with pens and pencils.

Instead, please use your hands to make your points:

- Gesture with them.
- Show measurements with them.
- Heft the weight of an imaginary object.
- Demonstrate movements.

You can open your hands. You can close them. You can plead with them. You can be adamant with them. You can look open with them. You can punctuate, count, or underline your ideas with them. In essence, use them in the same way that you do when you are having a conversation.

Another *caveat*: please don't point at members of the audience. Pointing may appear threatening or rude and is distracting. Beware of pointing not only with your finger, but also with a pen, pencil or pointer. Pounding the table is equally annoying, especially if you have an open microphone nearby.

See also
Q36   Why should I pay attention to my posture?
Q37   How can I use my head effectively?
Q41   Why should I become aware of and avoid distracting gestures?

Q41   Why should I become aware of and avoid distracting gestures?

Many of us have physical as well as verbal idiosyncrasies. Again, recall talks or lectures you have sat through during your lifetime. For example:

- Can you recall speakers repeatedly smoothing the seats of their trousers or straightening their ties?
- Can you recall speakers who fiddled with a button, pulled down a hem or pulled up a bra strap?
- Can you recall speakers who repeatedly twisted a stray strand of hair around an ear, or stroked their own faces, wiped their brows or pushed their sliding glasses back up their noses?

All these gestures are perfectly normal. But each of them can become problematic when they are repeated too frequently. The audience begins to focus on the nervous idiosyncrasies rather than on listening to your message.

See also

Q3   What can prevent communication?
Q4   How can I identify and eliminate my weaknesses as a speaker?
Q35   Is it better to stand still or move around?
Q36   Why should I pay attention to my posture?
Q40   What should I do with my arms and hands?
Q42   What does the audience notice about the way I move my feet?
Q54   How can I handle my own nervous reactions?

Q42   What does the audience notice about the way I move my feet?

Don't assume that the audience is looking only at your face and hands unless you are working remotely. In person, you should avoid being hidden by a lectern. You want the audience to see all of you, from your head to your feet. Unfortunately, many speakers rock back and forth on their toes. You may think no one will notice if you are standing behind a lectern. That isn't true. The audience can see your shoulders and head rise and fall as you rock.

In addition:

- Some speakers appear to be practicing dance steps.
- Still others look like new ice-skaters whose ankles keep bending.
- Some speakers slip their feet in and out of their shoes.
- Others try to polish their shoes by rubbing them against the backs of their trousers.

There's nothing wrong with any of these actions unless they are so frequent or creative that the audience becomes more intrigued by your foot movements than by your recommendations for change.

See also
Q40   What should I do with my arms and hands?
Q41   Why should I become aware of and avoid distracting gestures?
Q54   How can I handle my own nervous reactions?

Q43   Can my movements motivate the audience?

Although I encourage you to stand erect and look out at the audience, you will be more interesting and powerful as a speaker if you move around. You can motivate people to pay attention if you change position.

What kind of movement? If you are on a platform, you can walk to the left or to the right of where you originally started speaking. You can walk toward a corner of the room. You can move closer to some members of the audience. You can move up an aisle or down the side. When you do, your proximity may cause some people to feel mildly uncomfortable as you approach. But they concentrate on you again. Avoid getting so close that you are invading someone's personal space – just close enough to encourage them to refocus their attention on you.

When you move, you avoid pacing like a caged animal, or marching about like an irate teacher ready to catch someone texting. Move so that everyone can see and hear you and to create some additional interest.

Move to give expression to what you are saying. If you say, "... you can improve your chances of success by 5%, 10% or even 20% ... ," move a little to your left (or right) on "5%," a little more on "10%," and double the move on "20%." You will make your point visually as well as verbally.

See also
Q17   What motivational techniques can I use to grab the audience's attention?

Q35   Is it better to stand still or move around?

Q36   Why should I pay attention to my posture?

Q37   How can I use my head effectively?

Q40   What should I do with my arms and hands?

Q41   Why should I become aware of and avoid distracting gestures?

Q42   What does the audience notice about the way I move my feet?

Q48   How does altering the volume of my voice motivate the audience?

Q44   What should I consider when selecting what I wear?

Pick the outfit that you are going to wear in advance and be sure that it is clean and in good repair:

- Check to see that hems of skirts, trousers or jackets are not coming undone.
- Look for loose or missing buttons, and threads dangling down.
- Inspect for frayed collars, pockets or cuffs.
- Double-check for that soup stain on the front of a tie or blouse.
- Be sure that a pen has not leaked in your pocket.

Decide on an outfit that is appropriate for the occasion. Usually something simple or tailored is better. Ask yourself whether the pattern on the tie you selected is more interesting than what you are planning to say. If you are a woman, ask yourself whether your 2-inch earrings and décolletage are appropriate for this event or whether something less dramatic might be wiser.

Choose clothes that fit you. You don't need your collar to be too big for your neck or cuffs gathering at your ankles or sleeves sliding over those invaluable hands of yours. You don't need to wear socks that slip under your heels or to have ladders in your tights.

Choose a combination of colors that you believe is effective. Dark against light gives you the greatest contrast and therefore the greatest appearance of authority. If that is not the image that you want to project, then choose a softer combination, such as beige and blue. But make the decision in advance. Try to limit surprises. Color and comfort are equally important remotely so avoid fun patterns; keep it simple.

See also
Q16   How important is the audience's first impression of a speaker?
Q45   What should I consider when selecting my shoes?
Q46   What should I consider about the way I wear my hair?

Q45   What should I consider when selecting my shoes?

When presenting virtually, slippers or yoga socks may be fine; in person, not so much. Check to see whether your shoes are scuffed or are worn down at the heels. If they are, please clean or shine them or have them re-heeled. With polished shoes, you look more professional. You also look as if you care about your appearance and care about what the audience thinks.

Pick shoes that have no idiosyncrasies of their own. Some shoes love to squeak when you wear them. Others have wayward laces that enjoy becoming untied. Others have hard soles and make a noise as you walk to the podium or around the area.

Above all, pick shoes that are comfortable. You are going to be on your feet for a while when you give a talk or handle questions. Select shoes that don't hurt your feet after 15 minutes.

All this may sound obvious, but it is surprising how people inadvertently make the daunting task of speaking even harder by letting details undermine them.

See also

Q16   How important is the audience's first impression of a speaker?
Q44   What should I consider when selecting what I wear?
Q46   What should I consider about the way I wear my hair?

Q46 What should I consider about the way I wear my hair?

How you choose to dress for a talk is important. Remember that your audience looks at the whole person when you stand up, are introduced or walk to the front of the room. What you are wearing is part of the impression they form of you. That is equally true of virtual meetings.

Let's look at your hair:

- Maintaining eye-contact is essential to giving a successful talk, so if you have hair combed over one eye or constantly falling over your eyes, you will be unable to maintain eye-contact.

- If you have hair with a mind of its own that prefers to fall over your face, and you find yourself trying to put it back behind your ears, the gesture is distracting.

- If you are frequently swishing your head back like a horse tossing its mane, you are creating a distraction.

In essence, when you give a talk, choose a hairstyle that allows the audience to see your face. You don't want them spending time admiring your wonderful hair, marveling that it has a life of its own, and ignoring your ideas.

See also

Q16 How important is the audience's first impression of a speaker?
Q38 Why is eye contact key to effective presenting?
Q44 What should I consider when selecting what I wear?
Q45 What should I consider when selecting my shoes?

Q47   How rapidly should I speak?

Many speakers underestimate the importance of their vocal quality. In fact, most of us don't take full advantage of what that remarkable instrument – our voice – can do to enhance a presentation. The way you use your voice can make your talk more interesting.

As you know, we can speak both rapidly and slowly. We can also speak at a pace somewhere in between those two. Do so. Throughout your talk, vary the pace at which you speak. If you stay the same all the way through, then your talk becomes monotonous for the listeners. Speed up through sections or sentences that may be less vital to your central point. Slow down through more difficult passages or more important sections. You decide when and where.

Remember, most of us speak more rapidly at the beginning of a talk than we do later because we are more nervous at first. When you say your opening sentences, make a concerted effort to slow yourself down.

By the way, suppose you know that you have a strong regional accent, or you are speaking to a group whose native language is not your own, be sure that everyone can understand you. Again, the best method is to take it slower.

Making eye contact with your audience should tell you when you are losing them because you are speaking too quickly -- in person or remotely.

See also
Q48   How does altering the volume of my voice motivate the audience?
Q49   How can I discover whether I make unnecessary sounds when I speak?
Q50   Should I change my personality when I speak?
Q51   What is the power of pausing?
Q59   Should I use a microphone?

Q48   How does altering the volume of my voice motivate the audience?

Think of yourself as a sound system. You can adjust the volume, speak loudly and softly. If you speak at the same volume all the time, you become monotonous, as does speaking at the same speed throughout.

Know your own voice. If you have a big voice, and you are working in an intimate setting or remotely, your talk can become overbearing. Lowering the volume so that you speak softly may make people lean forward and pay more attention.

Using a microphone
There is no rule that says you must request a microphone when presenting in person. But, if you do use one, hopefully the organizers or you have one that permits freedom of movement. A clip-on may affect your clothing choice.

See also
Q47   How rapidly should I speak?
Q49   How can I discover whether I make unnecessary sounds when I speak?
Q51   What is the power of pausing?
Q59   Should I use a microphone?

Q49   How can I discover whether I make unnecessary sounds when I speak?

It is always good to record yourself once or twice so that you can play it back and listen to yourself. What should you pay attention to? Listen to the content of the talk. Also listen for sounds you make without realizing that you do. Sometimes we think out loud, so:

- Listen for "ems" and "ers."
- Listen for lip-smacking sounds.
- Listen for "tsk."

Some people press their tongues against the roofs of their mouths and then pull them away creating a kissing sound. Please understand that there is nothing inherently wrong with saying "em" or "er" or "tsk." But like so much of presenting, at some point the sounds may become a distraction. If you hear yourself making them, consider eliminating them. Like unnecessary gestures. the audience becomes more focused on the sound or gesture than on the message you want to share.

See also

Q50 Should I change my personality when I speak?

Speak naturally. Speak in a conversational tone. Yes, most of us would be delighted if we sounded like Judi Dench, Anthony Hopkins, or Kenneth Branagh in Shakespearean roles. No need. You are not giving sermons or soliloquies to the assembled masses. You are there to convince your colleagues of the merits of your arguments or recommendations. While it is true that much of presentation is theatrical, there is no need to intone or pontificate. Speak like a colleague.

However, that doesn't mean that you should be so relaxed and casual that you disregard the sound.

See also

Q1 What makes an effective speaker?
Q5 What are my strengths as a speaker?
Q54 How can I handle my own nervous reactions?
Q57 How can I build my confidence as a speaker?

Q51   What is the power of pausing?

One of the most effective ways of bringing home a point is by pausing. Pausing means stopping and waiting. For most of us, this is hard to do. We are uncomfortable with silence. But, when you pause, you allow your audience time to absorb your words or to reflect on what you have said or shown them.

How do you pause? Simply come to the end of a thought and wait. Pausing throughout your talk after key sections is effective. You decide when.

There is one time when you should always stop and pause: at the end of a talk. The pause is after your last sentence. Make your final remark. Wait. Then change your head or posture or your tone of voice. Then thank your audience or prepare to take questions. There should be a clear differentiation between your presentation and the closing amenities. Avoid letting your farewell interfere with your closing statements. Your powerful message may get lost.

See also
Q2   What are the steps in the communication process?
Q47   How rapidly should I speak?
Q48   How does altering the volume of my voice motivate the audience?

Q52   Why is enthusiasm essential?

Think about it. If you don't care about the subject matter of your talk, why should your audience? Whatever your topic and no matter how often you may have had to say what you are saying, you should sound fresh and enthusiastic. Presumably your words are new to your audience. Your face should look pleasant; your voice should sound it too. And you can put a smile in your voice.

Next time you make a phone call, listen to the way the person answers. Listen to the tone of voice. Some people sound as if they can barely make it through the day. Others sound as if they resent the interruption. Still others sound as if they are pleased to be at work and even more delighted to be hearing from you.

When you give a presentation, you can – and should – sound enthusiastic or committed to your subject matter, regardless of what it is that you are trying to explain to your audience. Be interested in your subject. If you are, the odds are that your audience will be too.

Even if they are having bad days, stage actors require as much energy for their performances on the 50th night as on opening night. We do, too. Trainers who have taught a course multiple times, or individuals who run induction meetings, know that they need to sound as if the material is new and exciting to motivate the audience.

See also
Q1   What makes an effective speaker?
Q50   Should I change my personality when I speak?
Q57   How can I build my confidence as a speaker?
Q94   What should I always try to do – hard as it seems?

Q53   Is stage fright normal?

Yes, stage fright is normal. Actors experience pounding hearts. Musicians face sweaty palms. Athletes have dry throats. The "jitters," "butterflies" or "stage fright" are perfectly normal experiences. Your adrenaline is flowing. Sometimes after an injection at the dentist's, you may notice that your hands shake and your heart races. You are experiencing an "adrenaline rush." When you do, you are more alert and ready to take on your opponent, to face the music and the audience. In fact, that anxious feeling does not last very long. It is an unusual person who is on edge throughout an entire talk.

If you think about the last time you spoke before a group or got ready to take part in a competition, you will recall that the adrenaline flowed to get you going. Then your talent, technique and preparation got you through the rest. You are nervous because you want to do well. You want to survive. You want a positive reception rather than appearing foolish. But usually within a minute or two, your heart stops racing, and your hands stop shaking as you move deeper into your prepared remarks. The beginning of a talk is when you are most worried. This is normal.

See also
Q4   How can I identify and eliminate my weaknesses as a speaker?
Q54   How can I handle my own nervous reactions?
Q55   How should I handle mistakes and surprises?
Q56   Are there proven ways to stay calm?
Q58   Why is it important to get to know the layout of the venue?
Q61   How important is rehearsing my talk?
Q89   How does attention to detail pay off?

Q54 How can I handle my own nervous reactions?

Each of us experiences nervousness differently. For some, their mouths go dry. For others, hands shake, or the palms of their hands become wet. Still others experience a flush. For others, stomachs feel rocky — the "butterflies." Still others feel weak in their legs. Recognize how your body reacts and anticipate what you feel when you are nervous.

Depending on how your nervousness manifests itself, there are ways of handling or overcoming it:

- If your mouth goes dry, have a glass of room-temperature water nearby to sip.

- If your hands shake, then have your materials prepared, so you are not reaching for notes, pens or slides in the opening seconds of your talk.

- If your stomach feels hollow, be sure that you avoid any extra caffeinated drinks before your talk. Frankly, that advice is true for all speakers. True, caffeine may heighten concentration, but it also heightens the jitters and acts as a diuretic. The latter may send you running to the loo when you have other more pressing concerns, like presenting your talk.

- If your legs feel weak, be sure that you know the route to the front of the room or be already sitting there when it is your turn to speak. You don't need to trip up a flight of steps because your legs are not working the way they normally do.

- Take some good deep breaths through your nose to calm yourself.

In addition to developing coping mechanisms for your nervousness, like having water nearby or avoiding extra coffee, there are other ways of handling your nerves. You can:

- Write down your opening remarks. That way, if you are anxious, you have prompts. You can read from your written words while your heart stops racing.

- Have your materials ready, so that all you need to do is push a button, click a remote, or reach for your marker.
- Take the focus off yourself at the beginning by asking the audience a question.
- Change the focus by immediately turning to write something on a flip chart or whiteboard. The audience will think about the question or look at the image or words rather than your hands.
- Have material "pre-flipped," or on the screen, or on a white board.
- Give the audience something to read.

No matter how often you speak, you will always experience some degree of stage fright. That anxiety will manifest itself in particular ways for you. Anticipate it and compensate for it. Given the unique nature of your talk, you may be able to create your own techniques. Experiment. What works for someone else may not work for you.

See also

Q34   What kind of notes should I use?
Q53   Is stage fright normal?
Q55   How should I handle mistakes and surprises?
Q57   How can I build my confidence as a speaker?
Q61   How important is rehearsing my talk?
Q89   How does attention to detail pay off?

Q55   How should I handle mistakes and surprises?

Mistakes happen. We are human. We lose our place. We mis-speak. We skip a sentence. We use the wrong name or word. The slide jams, the image freezes, the microphone stops working or someone comes in a wrong door. You can list more human or technical glitches.

What is important is to take the slip in your stride rather than trying to hide it, to cover it up and pretend that it didn't happen. Deal with the problem. Ask for a moment to correct it, if it is a technical problem. Smile. Joke, if you can. Don't blame anyone else. Everyone in the room has been in the same situation. Frankly, if you handle the problem well, you will enchant the audience. They will see you as human and credible.

That last remark is not suggesting that you deliberately make mistakes to win their approval, but if a problem arises, address it, rather than hide it.

By the way, an audience will accept one or two mistakes. but when errors occur too often, you risk alienating them. What appears to be an inadvertent slip-up suddenly looks like lack of preparation, and the audience may take offense.

See also
Q54   How can I handle my own nervous reactions?
Q56   Are there proven ways to stay calm?
Q58   Why is it important is it to get to know the layout of the venue?
Q61   How important is rehearsing my talk?
Q63   How can I limit mistakes?
Q64   How important is a dress rehearsal?
Q66   How can I prepare for questions?
Q89   How does attention to detail pay off?
Q94   What should I always try to do – hard as it seems?

Q56   How can I remain calm?

Be careful about drinking caffeinated drinks before you give a talk, because they heighten anxiety; however, be sure to eat. Speaking requires energy and food. You don't need to feel light-headed or headachy because you have skipped breakfast or lunch. On the other hand, don't overeat. What you don't need is to belch or to have indigestion.

Some people want to drink alcohol or take medication to calm down. You don't have the same kind of control of yourself when you do. Instead:

- Take deep breaths; let the oxygen calm your system.
- Think happy thoughts, as Peter Pan admonished us to do.
- Use relaxation techniques.
- Visualize calm images; think of peaceful scenes.

Think of a place that is quiet for you. It may be an empty seashore or a meadow of flowers or a furze-covered hillside. Find an image that is calming and recall it before you give your talk.

See also
Q54   How can I handle my own nervous reactions?
Q55   How should I handle mistakes and surprises?
Q57   How can I build my confidence as a speaker?

Q57   How can I build my confidence as a speaker?

One of the best ways of overcoming your nervousness is to remind yourself that you have something useful to share with the audience. Squelch the voices in your head telling you that you are going to make a mistake, that you are going to trip or forget what you had planned to say. Instead, tell yourself that what you have to say can make a difference to the people in front of you. Your ideas can affect their lives or their work.

Perhaps what you say will:

- Save the audience money or time.
- Make them feel better about themselves.
- Make them laugh or smile.
- Clarify or eliminate confusion.
- Help them to know more than they did before.

Regardless of what you are planning to say to the audience, before you begin, remind yourself of your value to that audience. That message may reassure a failing ego or a weakened sense of self-esteem.

See also
Q1   What makes an effective speaker?
Q5   What are my strengths as a speaker?
Q54   How can I handle my own nervous reactions?
Q58   Why is it important to get to know the layout of the venue?
Q61   How important is rehearsing my talk?
Q89   How does attention to detail pay off?
Q96   What should I reflect on when the presentation is over?
Q98   What kind of feedback should I seek to help to develop as a speaker?
Q100   What ongoing activities will help me become an effective speaker?

Q58   Why is it important to get to know the layout of the venue for an in person talk?

If you feel that your talk is a "me against them" contest, you may think of the venue as an arena. Or you may consider the presentation as a theatrical event, so the venue is a stage. Regardless of the name, it is the place where you will speak. The more you know about it, the more effective you will be.

One of the best ways to overcome your fear and to give an effective presentation is to check out the room in which you will be working. Visit the room in advance for a few minutes. If the location is far away, fly in early. If it is in another building, arrange to visit. If it is in your own offices, stop by early in the morning. But do visit the room. Walk around. Study it from all angles. Ask questions like:

- Where will I be sitting before I speak?
- Where will the audience be sitting?
- Where will I be speaking from?
- What is the walk like from my seat to the podium?
- Do I have to walk up or down any steps?
- Will I stand up from my seat to speak?
- Can everyone see me?
- How far am I from my audience?
- Will the audience be too comfortable on soft chairs or uncomfortable on metal seats?
- Do the chairs squeak?
- Are the floors carpeted, concrete or wooden?
- Where are the windows and doors?
- What are the acoustics like?
- Can people come in and out while I am speaking?
- Are there telephone extensions in the room? Will they ring?

- Are there wires or flexes on the floor? Can I or others trip over them?
- How is the audience arranged?
- Is there a lectern?
- What is the available technology – and do I know how to use it?
- Do I need IT support?

Be sure to survey the room in advance to anticipate any potential problems. And if you are working remotely, decide on the background, the lighting and how to handle potential puppy, cat or child invasions.

See also

Q59   Should I use a microphone?

Walk about the venue and check for the quality of the sound. Are there heavy curtains on the windows? Is the room heavily carpeted? If so, then you know that sound will be absorbed. If you find that the room is bare and the floors uncovered, then you may get an echo. Sometimes if you walk on a wooden floor, your footsteps will make more noise than you want.

Look up too. Ask these questions:

- Is the ceiling high?
- Will my voice be lost?
- What is on the other side of the wall?
- Are the walls thick? Are they temporary walls?
- What is scheduled next door during my talk?
- Are noises next door or in the area nearby likely to interrupt my talk?

Make sure that your audience will not be distracted, and they can hear you. What you learn from these quick checks will help you to determine whether you need to use a microphone.

Then find out the type of mic available and practice with it or reject it. A stationary microphone is just that – stationary. A handheld allows you to move, but fills your hands, while a clip-on gives you freedom, but may affect clothing choice.

See also
Q48   How does altering the volume of my voice motivate the audience?
Q60   What kind of set up do I need to ensure a smooth presentation?
Q65   Should I trust my equipment?
Q90   What should I check prior to speaking?

Q60   What kind of set up do I need to ensure a smooth presentation?

Examine the venue; then decide what you need to adjust and what you need to request from the organizers. In addition to surveying the room, speak to someone standing at the back and decide whether you will need a microphone. In a boardroom, it is unlikely that you will, but in a large conference room, you might.

Then check:

- Is the room arranged the way you want it to be?
- Do you need flipcharts, tables, screens or whiteboards? Are they already there?
- Is the flipchart on the correct side for you, depending on whether you are right- or left-handed?
- If you are bringing your own equipment, will you need extension cords, markers, erasers? Or will they be there waiting for you? Have you asked for them?
- If you are projecting slides or films, what are you projecting onto? Will the screen be down? Is it a pull-down screen? Can you reach it? Is it hand-pulled or does it operate electronically?
- Where are the switches for lights?
- Do you need a table for your materials? Is it the right size for you to put your materials on?
- Does the room get dark enough? Are there blinds? Can you see your own notes if all the lights are out?

In other words, once you have looked around the area in which you will be working, determine what you will need to eliminate problems and to enhance your work.

See also
Q59   Should I use a microphone?

Q61   How important is rehearsing my talk?

Most of us have had to practice at some time in our lives. If we sang, played an instrument or were involved in a sport, we had to practice. While many of us may not have liked the routine of the exercises, scales or drills, we knew we had to do them. What we wanted was to get on with the singing, the playing or the competing. But we knew that practice did make a difference in our performances. It is no different for speaking.

Practicing builds your confidence. If you are more confident, not only will you appear surer of yourself you also will be less nervous. Practicing for a talk consists of running through the talk to increase your familiarity with it and saying it out loud several times. Even if you only have time for two or three run-throughs, you become more at ease with your own words.

In addition, as you do your run-throughs, you may want to make some changes in the content. You may:

- See opportunities for emphasis or for pausing.
- Sense that sections drag or need to be cut a bit.
- Want to keep certain material but decide to speak quickly when you go over a less critical section.
- Discover you want to include a thought, an analogy or a story that you had forgotten to include.

Those changes, the decisions about delivery and your growing familiarity with your material, increase your sense of security.

Remember you are not committing your talk to memory. In fact, please don't! You may lose spontaneity when you do. But know your talk well enough so you are talking rather than reading.. You want your notes to be cue cards, rather than a script.

See also
Q34   What kind of notes should I use?
Q51   What is the power of pausing?
Q63   How can I limit mistakes?

Q64   How important is a dress rehearsal?
Q89   How does attention to detail pay off?
Q90   What should I check prior to speaking?

Q62   Why should I time myself?

When you practice, look at the time when you start and as you speak and when you finish. If you are scheduled to speak for 30 minutes, your talk should run slightly under 30 minutes, no longer. If you see that you are running over time, then you should make some adjustments to the content or the delivery.

Practice your talk aloud. The reason for doing this is that we do not read silently at the same pace that we read aloud. Certainly, reading to yourself increases your familiarity with your material, but reading aloud permits you to take pauses, to talk quickly or to slow down.

As you practice, imagine the audience reacting to what you are saying and plan for those reactions. Build in time for a laugh (or two) or a pause. If you are using visuals, allow time for the audience to look at what you are showing them. If you see that you are running over time in your rehearsal, you may consider eliminating some of your material – a decision better made beforehand than on the day.

See also
Q61   How important is rehearsing my talk?
Q73   What do I need to know about the length of my talk?
Q74   Why is awareness of time important?

Q63   How can I limit mistakes?

The more you practice, the fewer mistakes. You may make one or two, or none.

When you practice with your notes, when you listen to yourself, when you become increasingly more comfortable with what comes first or second, then you will find that you do not have to ask yourself, "What do I say next?" The segues will come more naturally.

In addition, you will be able to time yourself and be less concerned and more at ease with what you are doing. If you have a difficult section to deliver, you have the opportunity to run through that part several times just as you would within a difficult passage in music, or an awkward move in sports.

One good reason for practicing is to increase your comfort level with your material, thus limiting your mistakes and freeing you to concentrate on the audience's behavior, not on your own.

See also
Q55   How should I handle mistakes and surprises?
Q60   What kind of set up do I need to ensure a smooth presentation?
Q61   How important is rehearsing my talk?
Q64   How important is a dress rehearsal?
Q89   How does attention to detail pay off?
Q90   What should I check prior to speaking?

Q64   How important is a dress rehearsal?

If you can, arrange time to practice in the room in which you will be presenting. Up to now you may have been practicing in your office, in the bathroom, in a corridor, or in your living room. Now try to practice in the room you are going to be using for your talk.

Arrange to come in early or schedule a time with the organizers or the person who called the meeting to get into the room and practice. It doesn't matter if chairs are being set up while you are in there, just "do your thing." All you need is enough time to run through your talk at least once.

This will help you to:

- Get used to where you will be standing.

- Determine whether there is room to walk around.

- Check the sight lines to determine whether everyone can see you from every seat.

- Check the lighting to see whether there is any glare or whether you can read your notes.

- See whether blinds, curtains or shades need to be adjusted slightly to allow you to see the audience or for them to see your projected material.

- Sit in one of the audience's seats, shift your weight around in it and listen for noise.

- Test your voice by going to the front and saying a sentence or two while someone stands in the back. Ask whether you can be heard. Remember that when the room is filled, you will have to speak more loudly.

- Discover whether the room has any idiosyncrasies like columns, a noisy ventilation system, or a squeaky floorboard where you are standing.

- See whether any equipment you requested or brought has been set up and is working properly.

- Be sure that a flipchart has enough paper and is located where you want it positioned.

- Check that you have the right type and color markers for the flipchart or for a white board.

Although you may feel silly, give your talk in the room even if the room is empty. Move around. Check the time. A dress rehearsal makes a difference to your confidence.

See also

Q57   How can I build my confidence as a speaker?
Q60   What kind of set up do I need to ensure a smooth presentation?
Q61   How important is rehearsing my talk?
Q65   Should I trust my equipment?
Q89   How does attention to detail pay off?
Q90   What should I check prior to speaking?

Q65   Should I trust my equipment?

Be sure that you are familiar with your equipment, even if it is your own. You are a pilot checking your instruments before take-off.

Depending on what you are using, make your own mental checklist. It might include:

- Being sure that no one has borrowed a piece of equipment that you need.
- Double-checking for the location of power switches.
- Checking the extension cords.
- Testing the microphone.
- Finding the thermostat.
- Projecting an image to see if it's sharp or blurry.
- Having a call-in number if you are working remotely.
- Testing your computer.

Be sure that your equipment is placed in the right location so that any images that you are projecting fit clearly and neatly on the screen. You don't want legs cut off, or the last bullet point in a list projected on the wall below the screen. Sadly, good talks sometimes miss the mark because technical interruptions occur that could have been avoided with just a few minutes of preparation. We should be our own advance team.

See also
Q60   What kind of set up do I need to ensure a smooth presentation?
Q64   How important is a dress rehearsal?
Q89   How does attention to detail pay off?
Q90   What should I check prior to speaking?

Q66   How can I prepare for questions?

Sometimes, you can give a non-interactive talk – a lecture – from you to the audience; however, ideally your talk involves some exchange of ideas. That dialogue usually takes the form of questions. Therefore, a good presenter recognizes that it is essential to prepare both for the formal talk and for questions.

Probably the best way to prepare for any questions or for a formal question-and-answer (Q&A) session is to think about your audience once again. Remind yourself who will be present. Think again about their personalities and their job titles. When you do, you will begin to put yourself in their shoes and think from their perspectives. Depending on your subject, ask yourself some questions. Having heard your message, will people be concerned:

- About cost?
- About safety?
- About timeframe?
- About perceptions?
- About the long-term implications?
- About ease of access?
- About training?
- About necessary personnel?

In other words, consider how what you are planning to say might affect members of your audience or the people they represent. As you anticipate some of their questions, begin to formulate some of your answers.

In some instances, you may want to build some of your answers into your talk. You do that by saying something like, "Some of you may be wondering how we can implement such recommendations ..." or, "You may be concerned by the costs associated with this project, therefore ..."

In addition to anticipating questions yourself, you may prefer to have some questions posed by someone else — a colleague who will listen to your rehearsal and be willing to challenge your ideas. Questions "planted" like this are often used to get a discussion going – it's awkward when a Q&A session is met with silence.

Q67   How should I handle questions?

To answer questions well, listen to what is being asked of you. Avoid cutting off the questioners by answering before they are finished. In other words, do not finish the other person's sentence. Wait. Look at the individual and let the person pose the full question.

If the question is unclear, you may want to ask for clarification. You might say, "Do I understand you to mean ...?" or some similar phrase. Remember that your responses are part of your presentation as well. So, listen intently and politely.

Be sure that everyone in the room hears the question. Either ask the person to repeat the question for the group, or you can repeat it and answer it. For example, "Sam just asked if we will be ...," then answer the room, not just to the person who asked.

Sometimes, one of the organizers will act as a master of ceremonies (MC) and field the questions for you. In that instance, you simply wait for the MC to identify the questioner and then handle the questions in the same way that you would without an MC.

See also
Q66   How can I prepare for questions?
Q68   How should I answer questions?
Q69   How should I handle difficult or provocative questions?
Q70   How should I address tangential questions?
Q71   How should I treat a questioner?
Q91   How should I handle introductions?
Q97   How can I use the questions I was asked to improve my next talk?

Q68   How should I answer questions?

When you are asked a question, answer it. In political debates, we see politicians avoid awkward questions by restating their positions or by attacking a member of another party. But in most instances in business, there is no need to use such strategies. If you have the answer to the question, respond in an honest, straightforward manner. When you do, you gain the respect of the audience.

If you do not know the answer, if you do not have the figures at hand, or if you do not have the necessary data, say so. Your professionalism and credibility matter. Presumably you have put a good deal of time and effort into delivering a quality talk. It would be a shame if you damaged yourself by "waffling," making up statistics, or telling lies. We are not omniscient. Tell the questioners that you do not know the answer, or that you do not have the material with you. You can always provide it later. And, if you promise to send the material to them, be sure you do.

If you are unsure of a particular answer, you might turn to a colleague who has worked with you on the project and may recollect the specific data. But beware of putting someone else on the spot.

See also
Q66   How can I prepare for questions?
Q67   How should I handle questions?
Q69   How should I handle difficult or provocative questions?
Q70   How should I address tangential questions?
Q71   How should I treat a questioner?
Q91   How should I handle introductions?
Q97   How can I use the questions I was asked to improve my next talk?

Q69   How should I handle difficult or provocative questions?

There are times and any number of reasons why members of the audience may irritate you:

- They may ask questions that you think are unreasonable.
- They may be using the meeting as a forum for their own personal agendas.
- They may be trying to posture in front of someone else.
- They may want to appear invaluable.
- They may want to appear intelligent.
- They may be trying to show someone else up – or you for that matter.

Hard as it may be under these circumstances, stay calm. Usually what happens is that the people asking such tough, provocative or awkward questions undermine themselves in the eyes of the audience. Instead of seeming clever, they appear arrogant. Thus, the questions backfire, and the questioners end up seeming pompous, petulant or impertinent. Do not underestimate the awareness of the audience – they will recognize what is happening. When you are gracious, when you are patient, when you are charming, the other person looks foolish. Thus, there is no need to get into a shouting match. Take the high ground and repeat your position.

See also
Q66   How can I prepare for questions?
Q67   How should I handle questions?
Q68   How should I answer questions?
Q70   How should I address tangential questions?
Q71   How should I treat a questioner?
Q91   How should I handle introductions?
Q97   How can I use the questions I was asked to improve my next talk?

Q70   How should I address tangential questions?

During a question-and-answer session, it is easy to find yourself being asked tangential questions. Before long, you may realize that you have strayed far from your topic. It happens because one person poses a question, someone else picks it up, and then a third adds a follow-up. Before long, you may find yourself far afield responding to issues that are no longer relevant to your topic.

If that happens, take charge. To return to your subject, ask the audience if they have any questions about a particular aspect of what you were saying. In other words, redirect the audience back to your original message.

Keep your purpose in mind. Remember what you are trying to recommend or encourage, so bring your answers back to that message. It is important to stay focused, even though the formal part of the talk is over.

See also

Q71   How should I treat a questioner?

Asking questions is a form of mini-presentation. All eyes move away from the speaker to the person asking the question. When you attend a meeting or a conference and are asked if you have any questions, you spend time formulating your question. Quite simply:

- You want to avoid appearing stupid.
- You want to avoid asking a question that has already been asked.
- You want to avoid asking a question that has already been answered in the presentation, which suggests you weren't listening.

Such thoughts are in the minds of most questioners. You, as the speaker, should respect their anxiety. So, when you are asked questions, respect the people who ask them. They, not you, may be nervous now. Listen intently. Smile. Look pleased. If it is a thoughtful question, say so. In other words, respect any person who has the courage to ask you a question.

See also

Q66   How can I prepare for questions?
Q67   How should I handle questions?
Q68   How should I answer questions?
Q69   How should I handle difficult or provocative questions?
Q70   How should I address tangential questions?
Q91   How should I handle introductions?
Q97   How can I use the questions I was asked to improve my next talk?

Q72   Should I always accept a speaking opportunity?

Among the variables that contribute to creating a good presentation, time is one of the most important. It is a precious commodity for us all. Value your audience's time as well as your own.

Making presentations is a daunting prospect. We fear for our reputations. That healthy anxiety is why you should remember that if you are asked to present, you always can say "No."

One reason for declining might be because you do not feel confident enough about the topic. However, it is unlikely that you would be asked to speak on a subject if you lacked the knowledge.

Therefore, a main reason for saying "No" is the realization that you do not have enough time to prepare a good talk. Of course, in crisis situations, you may have little or no choice. But when you are asked to speak at a conference, a seminar or a meeting, before you jump at the opportunity for visibility, think about whether you have enough time to prepare adequately.

You need time to organize your thoughts, to design any supporting visuals and to practice. Therefore, if you feel that you cannot do justice to your topic, your company or yourself, decline the invitation or negotiate for a better time. Be realistic.

See also
Q1   What makes an effective speaker?
Q5   What are my strengths as a speaker?
Q60   What kind of set up do I need to ensure a smooth presentation?

Q73   What do I need to know about the length of my talk?

If you do decide to say "Yes" to giving a presentation, ask more questions. Besides determining the date of the presentation, find out how long your talk is supposed to be. Is it to be 30 minutes or 15 minutes? If you are told 30 minutes, ask if that includes questions or whether the question time is additional. If the question period follows your talk, then agree on how long that period will be. You want to plan for the exact amount of time that your session will be. Try to get specific answers rather than "Oh, about 20 minutes or so" or "around 30 minutes."

Many organizers are casual in their responses. For your own planning, try to determine exactly how much time you have. Having to cut essential material on the fly or to *ad lib* simply to fill the unplanned time now available is an additional stressor.

See also

Q62   Why should I time myself?
Q74   Why is awareness of time important?
Q75   What are the implications of "when" I speak?
Q76   Why should I try to pick my "slot" at a conference?

Q74   Why is awareness of time important?

You have been there. You have sat through talks that have gone on longer than expected. You were led to believe you would be listening to a five-minute analysis, and 20 minutes later the individual is still talking.

As a speaker, avoid running long. Wear a watch, or have a phone or computer or clock within sight – and practice your talk in advance. You want to finish your presentation on schedule – that alone will impress the audience.

People in the audience have expectations and responsibilities. If you say that you are going to spend the next five minutes explaining, then be sure that it is five minutes, not 10. If you begin by indicating that "in 20 minutes, all of you will feel more comfortable with ...," you have set up expectations.. They expect 20 minutes, not 15 and certainly not 25. Keep your word. They will appreciate your sensitivity to their obligations. They will concentrate. They also will stay. People leaving a virtual or live meeting while someone is speaking is distracting – so pause.

See also
Q62   Why should I time myself?

Q75   What are the implications of "when" I speak?

When you are asked to give a talk, think about when that talk is scheduled for: the time of the day, the time of the week, and the time of the year. In other words, if you are asked to speak at 10 am, your delivery might be different from a talk you might give at 8 pm. You might need to summon more energy at night, because you and your audience are tired. Asynchronous remote work complicates your efforts even more.

The same is true for different days. A talk on a Monday at 8:00 am is different from one given on a Wednesday at the same time or one given on a Friday. On Monday, people may be refocusing from the weekend, and on Friday the weekend may be uppermost in their thoughts. .

Consider too, what else is happening in the office or in the world:

- Are you scheduled to speak at the same time as a major sporting event, election or impending holiday? Is it the World Cup or a bank holiday?
- Are people more concerned with a rugby final than they are with what you have to say?
- Are you competing with people's attention for holiday parties?

So, think about the "when" before you accept the offer to speak. If you do opt to present even though there is a major event happening simultaneously, you may have to modify your presentation style based on what that conflict or event is. In other words, consider the implications of your time slot.

See also
Q3   What can prevent communication?
Q72   Should I always accept a speaking opportunity?
Q73   What do I need to know about the length of my talk?
Q76   Why should I try to pick my "slot" at a conference?

Q76 Why should I try to pick my "slot" at a conference?

Probably you will be speaking to small groups of co-workers, at a meeting with a client, or in your own boardroom. However, there will be times when you will speak to a large group at a conference.

It is wonderful to be invited to speak because you have been identified as someone with something to say. But beware of being so flattered by the honor of being approached that you allow yourself to be railroaded into being scheduled randomly by the organizers.

When you are invited to speak, be sure that you negotiate for the best slot for yourself. If you know that you are more alert in the morning than in the afternoon, then request an early slot. Conversely, if you know that you are more alert in the afternoon, ask for time in the afternoon. Do not be bashful. Remember you are valuable for the organizer. It is in your best interests to make the request.

Before you agree to speak right after lunch, consider that slot well. Some people call it the "black hole." One reason is that lunches at conferences are usually heavy-going. People may be sleepy. They may have been socializing over dessert and are reluctant to stop chatting with new-found colleagues.

Either way, they may be inattentive. If you do agree to speak after lunch, design your talk accordingly. You may have to liven or lighten up your talk. In other words, your time slot and its relationship to other speakers are important for you.

See also
Q3 What can prevent communication?
Q75 What are the implications of "when" I speak?
Q77 Why should I find out who else is speaking at a conference?

Q77   Why should I find out who else is speaking at a conference?

If you are speaking at a conference, there will be other speakers. Find out who they are and when they will speak.

Ask the name of the keynote speaker, if it is not you. Find out when that individual will be speaking and decide if you want to precede or follow. Some keynote speakers are exciting; others are not, but you should avoid being viewed as a warm-up act or, worse yet, as an afterthought to the highlight of the day.

And find out the subject matter of the keynote speaker and the others. Know their subjects or perspectives because it is helpful to know that you will be saying something similar to or contradictory to someone else, so you can alter your remarks accordingly.

See also
Q76   Why should I try to pick my "slot" at a conference?
Q78   How can I benefit by listening to other speakers at a conference?

Q78   How can I benefit by listening to other speakers at a conference?

On the day, try to arrange to listen to the other speakers, certainly to the ones ahead of you and, if possible, to those who follow. You may be unable to rearrange your schedule but do try to hear the people who precede you. It is valuable for you to hear what other people say so that you can modify your own thoughts.

When you listen to other speakers:

- You may find that someone is opposed to your notions and is contradicting everything you plan to say.
- You may find that someone has a similar position on one aspect of your talk.
- You may find that someone is dead wrong about something.
- You may find that someone uses a clever approach that charms the audience.

If you listen, you may find that you can make minor adjustments or take advantage of what you have heard to enhance your own talk. There is no reason why you can't say, "Despite my colleague's enthusiasm for ...," "I want to express my delight that John said ..." or, "Phyllis' reference to traffic reminds me of ..." You are showing that you listen and are also using the other speakers' words to reinforce or underline your own message.

See also
Q77   Why should I find out who else is speaking at a conference?

Q79   What is essential for an effective team presentation?

Preparing for a team presentation is different from working as a lone speaker. For a team presentation to appear professional, work together. Once you know what your topic is, discuss among yourselves who in the group will handle which section.

In your deliberations:

- Decide whether one of you is stronger in an area or if one of you is new to the material.
- Decide who will speak for how long.
- Decide who will speak first.
- Decide who will make the introductions.
- Decide how you will move from one speaker to the next.

You also might consider which one of you will assist with any materials you plan to use. For example, do flipchart pages need to be turned? Do hand-outs need to be distributed? Do you need assistance recording or moving to the next slide? Rather than the speaker handling the technology, a team member could be responsible until it is their turn.

Another item to plan together is the handling of questions. Perhaps one of you wants to answer all of them. Or maybe you want to divide the subject matter into sections and have the person who spoke on that subject answer the questions relating to it.

In essence, find the time in advance of the presentation to discuss how you are dividing the tasks.

See also
Q80   What is a key requirement for a team presentation?
Q81   What makes a team presentation appear seamless?

Q80   What is a key requirement for a team presentation?

Just as you would if you were performing alone, as a member of a team you should find the time to work together. It looks bad when a group looks at each other anxiously, trying to make spontaneous decisions about what to do next. The decisions should have been made earlier. In person:

- You should know where you are going to be seated or be standing.
- You should know how you are going to get to your places.

Determine how you are going to introduce your colleague without using the hackneyed expression, "Now, I will hand it over to ..." Find a more creative and integrated way of moving to the next speaker: "Ethel will now clarify why ..." or "Stephen will walk you through the findings."

Once again, the presentation should look like a package: smooth and wrapped up. If the first person began the talk with a question, the final speaker should recall that question. In essence, your opening phraseology or approach should be echoed in the ending. If you decide to develop a mnemonic, it should be used throughout the talk, not just by the second speaker.

Practicing together increases your awareness of your differing styles. Thus, you will be able to pace yourselves and alter your individual sections to complement each other. Virtual teams should make most of the same decisions.

See also
Q61   How important is rehearsing my talk?
Q64   How important is a dress rehearsal?
Q79   What is essential for an effective team presentation?
Q81   What makes a team presentation appear seamless?

Q81   What makes a team presentation appear seamless?

It is remarkable how often team presentations still look like individual presentations given one right after another. If you are a team, the people who are waiting their turns should be:

- Paying attention to the speaker.
- Reacting to what the other person is saying.
- Sensitive to an error.
- Ready to stand in.
- Able to correct a technical problem.

Too often, the speakers who have gone first are so relieved to have survived the ordeal that they sigh, let their shoulders sag and look totally uninterested in what their colleagues are saying. Sometimes, in person, they even talk to team members seated next to them.

For the audience to be attentive to the talk, you should be too. Think about paintings you have seen in which there is a central figure with several others positioned around him or her. All eyes are directed toward that figure. The artist is directing you, the viewer, by having attention focused on the main person.

In the same way, consider yourself part of the piece of artwork. When you are silent, your attention should be on the speaker. Nod in agreement or smile when a joke is told. Remember you are a team – rather than a group of individuals. Your visual commitment to your colleagues pays off. When audiences see that you are paying attention to the speech, they will too.

Q82   Does every presentation need visuals?

Your visuals may include: slides, product samples, hand-outs, videos – to name a few options. Some speakers believe that visuals are an essential part of every presentation. That is not necessarily true. Such people assume it is essential because they see other speakers use PowerPoint all the time. You do not always need to include visuals in your talk. In fact, they can interfere. "Death by PowerPoint" is a reality. Sadly, visuals often are overused at the cost of the human relationship between speaker and audience.

Before deciding on whether to use visuals, think about the nature of your talk. Think about the message or messages that you want to get across. Think about the complexity of your ideas. Are you discussing a subject that is abstract or one that includes many calculations? These are two instances when having visuals might clarify your point or might reinforce your ideas.

Go through your talk and decide what aspects would benefit from some sort of visual reinforcement. Think about your options and decide what will help you get your message across:

- Should everyone have a copy of the budget?
- Would a pie chart or bar graph make your ideas clearer?
- Would three key points on a slide emphasize your main points?
- Would a photograph help?
- Would a column of numbers on a flipchart clarify your analysis?
- Would a product sample or model make a difference?
- Would a set of figures from a report explain your point?
- Should you show a video or play a recording to reinforce?

If your message is simple, you may need none.

See also
Q83   What is essential when I design or select visuals?
Q84   How do I incorporate visuals effectively?
Q85   How can a visual hurt my presentation?

Q83   What is essential when I design or select visuals?

If you decide to use visuals, remember your audience. Visuals are designed for the audience, not for you. Sometimes, speaker use slides as if they were cue cards for themselves in place of using another form of note. Such visuals are designed for the presenter rather than the audience.

If you do decide to use visuals:

- Consider the nature of the room and the size and composition of the group. Be sure that everyone in every seat can see every letter or picture that you show them. If virtual, remember staring at a complicated slide adds to the fatigue.

- Keep your images simple. Everyone should be able to see what you have written without squinting. Multiple paragraphs with 10 or 12 sentences are hard to read.

- Keep your bullet points consistent. If you begin the first one with a verb, then have the others start with a verb. If your bullets begin with nouns, then all of them should begin with nouns.

- The audience will have trouble deciphering slides and transparencies that are overloaded with numbers or graphs.

- Avoid actual pages of reports on a screen because they are hard to read.

- Avoid using all bold because if the visuals confuse, they are not serving your purpose.

- Think about color choices. Some folks have difficulty with red and green, and pastels may be, well, too pastel.

In addition, be sure that your choice of visual is appropriate for the group. Sometimes, cartoons or photographs appeal to a certain segment of your audience but not to the whole group. As with so much of presentation, make careful decisions and remember that often "less is more."

See also
Q82 Does every presentation need visuals?
Q84 How do I incorporate visuals effectively?
Q85 How can a visual hurt my presentation?

Q84   How do I incorporate visuals effectively?

If you project a visual on a screen, the audience may look at any part of the projected image. Help them. Guide them by telling them where to look. "If you look at the lower half of the screen …," "Please look at the segment on the pie chart which represents 25 per cent," or "Let me direct you to the second paragraph …" Each of these phrases helps the audience to stay with you. Of course, you can point, but laser pointers are not popular with everyone for many reasons, the least of which is that they can be distracting. Your finger or a pointer may be offensive or may shake. Words are often the best way to direct your listeners.

Beware of falling into the trap of turning to point out something on the screen. You will discover that your back is completely turned to the audience, and your voice is projected toward the screen rather than out into the room. You also have lost eye-contact with your audience. You can face forward and use your right or left arm and hand to show them where to look.

See also

Q82   Does every presentation need visuals?
Q83   What is essential when I design or select visuals?
Q85   How can a visual hurt my presentation?

Q85   How can a visual hurt my presentation?

Nothing can kill a good presentation faster than an error on a visual. People enjoy finding spelling or grammatical errors. The trouble is that they begin to look for more errors or question the accuracy of your other figures. Be sure that what you have prepared is accurate and correct. Be sure that the spelling is "despair" and not "dispair." Be sure that you meant "it's" and not "its." Check that you meant "their" instead of "there." Check the spelling of names and the accuracy of dates.

In addition to the correct spelling and dates, put titles on your graphs and charts. Again, your audience may not be concentrating all the time or present from the start of your talk. If you put a title on a chart, you help the audience follow you and remember.

See also
Q82   Does every presentation need visuals?
Q83   What is essential when I design or select visuals?
Q84   How do I incorporate visuals effectively?

Q86   How should I use handouts?

While you may have emailed a PDF in advance to participants, handouts are wonderful if you want people to have the opportunity to recall what you have said when you and they are no longer together. They are also an excellent place for your audience to write notes, so leave enough white space.

However, if you do not control when and how you are going to use papers, they can be a nuisance. When you distribute them is important. If you leave handouts on chairs or on tables before you talk, people will begin to read then. In fact, you may find that they are reading them as you are talking. Sometimes it is better to wait until you have begun your talk to distribute them and then to guide the audience through their use as you would your other images. When you time your run-through, remember to include the distribution of samples or handouts. They add time.

See also
Q82   Does every presentation need visuals?

Q87   How can I ensure my credibility as a speaker?

It is all well and good to talk about specific issues like saying "em," putting your hand in your pocket or selecting the font for your visuals. However, there are other aspects to making a presentation that are more elusive.

Be honest. In this instance, "being honest" means being careful to avoid stretching the truth. Sometimes, in your desire to give a good presentation, you may make remarks that are less than 100 per cent accurate or validated. It can happen if you have had to prepare your presentation on a tight deadline. Despite your best efforts, you may lack all the data that you need to support your arguments. Thus, what you have may be incomplete. If that is the case, rather than letting the audience make assumptions, tell them at the outset what your limitations or your parameters are. Say "I will not be discussing ..." or, "I will be focusing only on ... " Refrain from presenting your material as if it were a complete and thorough analysis, if it is not.

"Why is this necessary?" you ask. Your good name and credibility are at stake if you are caught in a lie or even in a minor misrepresentation. If you say that "Everyone agreed that ..." when you lack the data to substantiate your conclusions and recommendations, then the audience may doubt your ideas. If one aspect of your work is suspect, then the accuracy of your findings and ultimately the wisdom of your recommendations may be called into question.

To repeat, your reputation and your organization's are on the line. The value of your good name cannot be measured, and it is difficult to repair once damaged. Protect yourself and your organization by providing accurate information.

See also
Q1   What makes an effective speaker?
Q3   What can prevent communication?
Q4   How can I identify and eliminate my weaknesses as a speaker?

Q5 What are my strengths as a speaker?
Q57 How can I build my confidence as a speaker?
Q96 What should I reflect on when the presentation is over?
Q100 What ongoing activities will help me become an effective speaker?

Q88 Which personal attribute is essential to all presentations?

We have all experienced times when we are put off by other people's behavior. Have you ever entered a new country, walked through immigration or customs and found yourself wondering what crime you have committed or are suspected of carrying out? Or have you entered a country and been greeted by a smiling, pleasant officer who welcomes you? Amazing how that smile makes a difference. In the first situation you may feel demeaned; in the second, you feel good.

The same is true for presentations. Speakers who:

- Appear cold seem to be indifferent.
- Never smile may appear unapproachable.
- Never look at their audiences may appear bored.
- Never make eye contact or who look out the window or at the back wall may appear aloof.

To motivate the audience to be interested in you and your words, your demeanor matters. Audiences want you to be enjoying the opportunity to be with them – regardless of the subject matter.

Convey empathy or sympathy, not only in your words, but in your smile. Laugh if the occasion warrants it. Gesture. Nod your head. If you make an error, laugh at yourself. Make the correction and take it in your stride. In sum, show with simple facial expressions or behaviors that you are a human being.

See also

Q89 How does attention to detail pay off?

Demonstrate to the audience that you care about them and your topic. The best way to do this is to take time preparing your presentation and paying attention to detail. Give a professional presentation. Show them that their opinion of you matters, too.

Make sure you:

- Check your work for errors of any kind.
- Have the correct spelling and pronunciation of names.
- Handle your material with pride.

Some speakers start by unfolding crumpled notes. Others toss their notes on the table as they finish. Still others leave their materials strewn around after a talk, as if those slides or samples were of no consequence to anyone. These gestures suggest a cavalier attitude. Instead, those materials should matter to you; they represent hours of work.

Be aware of what is happening around you and react. Be attentive to every question you are asked. Engage with the questioner. Listen intently and respond with enthusiasm to the questioner and to the audience, so you will be viewed as a concerned and committed professional.

See also
Q3 What can prevent communication?
Q55 How should I handle mistakes and surprises?
Q63 How can I limit mistakes?
Q87 How can I ensure my credibility as a speaker?
Q88 Which personal attribute is essential to all presentations?
Q90 What should I check prior to speaking?

ON THE DAY

Q90   What should I check prior to speaking?

Eventually, the day arrives. Up until now, you have been assembling and organizing your material. You also have practiced the actual delivery. Now it's different. You are facing the actual moment. This time your run-through is not for timing or emphasis. It is the real thing. It is show time!

For an in person talk, hopefully, you have already checked the room for the acoustics and the layout. On the day, however, you would do well to arrive early to check it once more. The fewer surprises the better. The markers you need are there, the lectern has been moved. The power is working, as is the thermostat.

When you carry out your check, be sure that:

- You know where any wires or flexes are lying in your path.
- The chairs are organized the way you thought they would be.
- No loud event is scheduled for the room next door, like a party, construction work, or a show.
- The room is light or dark enough for you to use your equipment or read your notes.
- Your equipment is working.
- Your water is accessible but away from any equipment.
- You check the sight lines again to be sure that everyone can see you and your visuals, and you can see them
- You can see over a lectern if you are using one. You don't want the audience to see only a talking head.
- You test the microphones and know where the on and off buttons are.

If a meal will be served while you are speaking, be prepared to pause while dishes are served or removed, or sandwiches unwrapped.

Look at the thermostat (if there is one in the room) to be sure that the room is neither too hot nor too cold. Open a window if the room is too hot or stuffy. If you can't adjust the temperature, you may have to adapt your presentation to the audience's physical comfort.

You get the idea. Survey the area. The more often you give presentations, the speedier the survey. While the details will differ for every talk, and each room has its own idiosyncrasies, you will discover that a brief survey eliminates surprises – the last thing a speaker needs.

See also
Q58   Why is it important to get to know the layout of the venue?
Q60   What kind of set up do I need to ensure a smooth presentation?
Q64   How important is a dress rehearsal?
Q65   Should I trust my equipment?
Q89   How does attention to detail pay off?

Q91   How should I handle introductions?

The devil is in the details. Find out whether you are introducing yourself or being introduced by someone else. Sometimes you may prefer to incorporate your own introduction into your opening remarks. On other occasions, you may prefer to have someone else introduce you.

In the first instance, you may want to explain why your experience qualifies you to speak on the subject.

If you are being introduced by someone else, be sure the introduction is the one that you want. Sometimes, the person making the introduction is inaccurate about your background or about your presentation. Be sure that their remarks are both true and correct. MCs have been known to indicate that the speaker is going to talk about one subject when the topic is not what the speaker intended talking about at all. The audience – never mind the speaker – ends up bewildered and/or disappointed.

Sometimes, the MC may give away too much. "Today John will be showing us a video of the new ...". Well, maybe you wanted the video to be a surprise. That's why it is important you compare notes with the MC beforehand.

Be sure that you know the name and the correct pronunciation of the person who is introducing you. It is polite and gracious for you to say the person's name, rather than just saying, "Thank you for the introduction".

Be sure that there are no changes in the seating arrangements. You may have planned to be seated at the front, but the organizer has placed you on a platform at the front of the room. In addition, ask the organizer whether you are going to be selecting questioners or if someone else will be recognizing people for you.

See also
Q17   What motivational techniques can I use to grab the audience's attention?
Q28   How should I handle courtesies like "thank you"?

Q66 How can I prepare for questions?
Q67 How should I handle questions?
Q68 How should I answer questions?
Q69 How should I handle difficult or provocative questions?
Q70 How should I address tangential questions?
Q71 How should I treat a questioner?

Q92   How should I handle problems during my presentation?

Mishaps occur. You skip a line. You mispronounce a word. You forget to move to the next slide. A bulb burns out. There is a squeal over the microphone. Your stomach grumbles. You sneeze. Whatever it is, it is not the end of the world. However, if you try to over-compensate or hide the slip or *faux pas* , it may become a problem. Rather than sympathizing with you, the audience becomes uncomfortable for you.

Do what you normally do in the situation. If you sneeze or cough, excuse yourself. If you need a drink of water, have one. If you lose your place, smile and find it. More than likely the audience will be charmed by the fact that you are human too.

This remark is not suggesting that you should deliberately make a mistake or be blasé about the audience's perception of you if you make many errors. While the audience may be charmed by your losing your place or train of thought once, they may become resentful or impatient if you do so three or four times. Naturally, they may wonder whether you value them and how much time you spent preparing your presentation.

See also
Q55   How should I handle mistakes and surprises?
Q63   How can I limit mistakes?
Q89   How does attention to detail pay off?
Q90   What should I check prior to speaking?

Q93   What can I do if I seem to be losing my audience?

You have a plan. And we all know about "the best laid plans;" they can and do go awry. You will have to react spontaneously to the situation. Remember that one of the reasons you are making eye-contact is so that you can see what is happening in front of you.

You will have to change your plan in some way if the audience:

- Is getting tired.
- Look bewildered.
- Appear not to hear.
- Didn't get your joke.
- Is turning to each other for clarification.

If heads are turned, stop. Look where the audience is looking to find out what is happening. Suppose everyone is staring at a door to your right. You cannot keep on talking. Look at the door and see what is going on. Perhaps someone is trying to come in. There could be someone signaling to a friend in the room. Handle whatever happens.

If you see people leaning forward with their heads cocked as if to hear you better, you may have to speak louder. If people look bored, you may have to speed up, slow down, stop – do something. If people look confused, you may have to repeat what you said or offer some clarification.

In other words, the audience's behavior on the day may tell you that you should make a change to ensure that they pay attention. It is all well and good wanting to get through your presentation, but remember your objective is to be sure that the audience hears and comprehends your message.

See also
Q87   How can I ensure my credibility as a speaker?
Q88   Which personal attribute is essential to all presentations?
Q92   How should I handle problems during my presentation?

Q94   What should I always try to do – hard as it seems?

Once you are over the jitters that you will most likely be experiencing in the first few minutes, enjoy what you are doing.

Think about it. Speaking to a group means you have an opportunity to make a difference to other people's lives. Smile, look around and react to what is going on – virtually or in person. So:

- If you recall a joke while you are speaking, you might work it in.
- If you can remember an anecdote that might serve as a case study to clarify your point, tell it.
- When you speak, remember to smile, to move around, to use your arms and hands. Be animated.
- If something unusual happens while you are speaking – the lights go out, a phone rings, a bird flies in the window, someone makes a telling or amusing comment – enjoy the moment, and laugh if it is appropriate.

Of course, if your presentation is on a painful subject, you would be hard pressed to enjoy yourself. But view the situation as an opportunity to make a change. They are usually opportunities for you to motivate your listeners. Your joy, humanity and enthusiasm should be contagious.

See also
Q1   What makes an effective speaker?
Q2   What are the steps in the communication process?
Q100 What ongoing activities will help me become an effective speaker?

AFTERWARDS

Q95   How should I feel when it is done?

Believe it or not, there will come a time when the talk is over. The questions have stopped. You have been thanked and have returned to your seat or are preparing to leave the meeting. But for a good speaker, it should not be over.

Be pleased with what you have done. Your talk may not have been perfect. You may have made a mistake. You may not have handled a question as well as you wanted to do. Nevertheless, be pleased. We are all excellent at finding fault with what we do. So, please do not resume your seat, wipe your brow, look down, and shake your head in disgust. We are our worst critics, and the audience may feel differently about your work on their behalf.

You should look pleased or confident. The truth is that you should be. Why? You worked hard. You have done your homework. You have prepared. You have practiced. You have survived a highly stressful experience. Be proud of yourself for doing that. Accept the fact that, every time you present, you will want to change some aspect of what you did. Speaking is an evolutionary process.

See also
Q1   What makes an effective speaker?
Q96   What should I reflect on when the presentation is over?
Q98   What kind of feedback should I seek to help to develop as a speaker?

Q96 What should I reflect on when the presentation is over?

To improve, learn from what you did. Certainly, you can berate yourself. You can applaud yourself too. To develop your skills, accept the applause from the audience, or the thanks from your host. Take some time to reflect on what you did and what you might have done or will do differently.

Over the next few hours or days, think about your talk from beginning to end. You can determine some of that by reflecting on the audience's reaction. What would you do again? What might you omit? Ask yourself whether you lost the audience at any point? Were there avoidable disruptions? Did any of the changes in the venue surprise you? Could any technical difficulties have been avoided? How did you handle them? Did you lose time because of a late start or a lengthy introduction? Did you need to cut material? Did you run long?

Think back:

- Did everyone laugh at your jokes or relate to your stories? Did you tell too many? Were they all appropriate?

- Did you find yourself going off at a tangent? Ask yourself how that happened.

- Do you think that all the visuals were effective? Ask yourself which ones worked.

- Did the talk flow naturally, or in retrospect, would you have eliminated some points and added others?

Would you decline an invitation for such a time or in such circumstances, if you were asked again?

See also
Q97 How can I use the questions I was asked to improve my next talk?
Q98 What kind of feedback should I seek to help to develop as a speaker?
Q100 What ongoing activities will help me become an effective speaker?

Q97   How can I use the questions I was asked to improve my next talk?

Whether you designed your speech to take questions along the way or at the end, the questions you were asked offer invaluable feedback for future talks. Did a question interrupt the flow? Did it reveal confusion and call for clarification? Did that question cause you to consider whether a different format might have been more effective?

But more importantly, what did the questions reveal? About your talk? About the audience? Were they, in fact, questions or statements? Did a question suggest that you might need to incorporate a point you hadn't made? Did a question help you to identify an objection to your message? What was the tone of the question? Did the question spark another idea for the future? Did you spend too much time on topics that the audience already understood?

Try to remember as many questions as you can or, if possible, consider recording them – though this may risk inhibiting the audience.

See also
Q13   How can I anticipate objections to my message?
Q67   How should I handle questions?
Q68   How should I answer questions?
Q91   How should I handle introductions?

Q98 What kind of feedback should I seek to help to develop as a speaker?

In addition to doing your own reflecting on the event, ask colleagues whom you trust what they thought. Ask members of the audience.

When they tell you that you were "super" or "grand," be wary. Being told that they "thoroughly enjoyed it" or that you were "marvelous" does not teach you anything. Sure, those comments may make you feel good, but specifics are more useful.

You will have to probe and ask "Why?" and "How?" The information will help you modify what you do for the next presentation.

In addition, evaluate the outcome. Did you get the new client? Did your staff do what you want? Did the board consider your recommendations? In other words, was your message taken seriously and acted upon, or were you ignored?

Q99   Can I give the same talk a second, or third, time?

Yes – and no. Certainly, if your talk is posted on social media and available on YouTube, it's a problem giving the same talk, but more likely than not, a second, or third audience may not have heard it before and won't know that you are repeating yourself. This is especially true of departmental Zoom meetings.

Unless your subsequent audiences are composed of exactly the same people as your first, you may change your talk, however slightly. Even if the core message and most of your talk is the same, you should alter the acknowledgements, and any local or current references, to fit the new audience. In any case, as suggested earlier, you should think about and learn as much as possible about the audience and their concerns so that even though the body of your talk or the sequence of your points may be the same, the opening analogies or objectives or hook may be different. Tailor your talk to each new audience.

For example, if your audience consists primarily of senior management, they may have greater concerns about the impact of your proposals on the bottom line than middle managers who may be more concerned with implementation, while new staff may have a greater interest in simply grasping the immediate implications for their learning curve. Usually, the opening and closing may vary significantly for the different audiences.

See also
Q7   What do I need to know about the audience?
Q8   Who should I address my talk to?
Q9   Why is the audience attending my talk?
Q10   How can I benefit from analyzing the relationships among the audience members?

Q100   What ongoing activities will help me become an effective speaker?

Besides reflecting on what you did and asking your colleagues what worked, watch other speakers. Find opportunities to do that. You can:

- Watch them on television.
- Look at them at the cinema.
- Attend talks, sermons, seminars and lectures.
- Check social media.
- Notice effective speakers in person or virtual meetings.

Watch and learn from what you are seeing and hearing. Study other people's techniques:

- Watch how someone moves and how the audience reacts.
- Notice how speakers use their voices.
- Notice the speaker's choice of clothing.
- Look for the speaker's idiosyncrasies.
- Evaluate the creative use of slides, handouts, samples or models.
- See what the speaker does to keep the audience's attention.

And, watch the audience. Pay attention to how the audience responds. Look around. Notice if side conversations are taking place. Notice if the audience is attentive, falling asleep or daydreaming. Notice if they are taking notes or checking phones. Ask yourself why whatever is happening is happening. Then consider what the speaker might do or might have done to change the outcome. Experiment.

Bear in mind, however, we are all individuals and what works for you as a speaker may not work for someone else, and *vice versa*. You may have seen someone burst balloons or pound a table, but that's alien to you. Reflect on what you see and select only those techniques with which you are comfortable – for example:

- Perhaps you do not stop or pause enough.

- Perhaps you could vary your speed.

- Perhaps you should stop talking more often when you use visuals.

- Perhaps you want more images and less talk.

- Perhaps you should try a mnemonic or have the audience engage in activities.

Look for opportunities to talk. The more often you speak, the more adept you become. Learning to be an excellent speaker is like learning any other new skill. Work on one aspect of presenting at a time. For example, you may want to focus first on your voice or on improving your posture. When you feel that you have made some changes, then work on another aspect. Perhaps you think that you could use your hands more effectively. Maybe you want to organize your thoughts differently. Work on that next.

In other words, identify each of your strengths as a speaker. Be conscious of them and use them. Then, identify weaknesses and eliminate them one at a time. The initial nervousness usually stays – but the dread will go. Your confidence will grow, too, as you have more and more of these experiences behind you. You will recognize that you can give a good presentation. Certainly, you will know that the floor will not open and swallow you. You also know that you can make a difference to your audience.

Find opportunities to talk. Even if it is only for five minutes, or even 10, speak. The more you do, the better you become. The more frequently you plan, speak and reflect on your audience's reaction the better. It is for your own development. The more often you speak, the more effective you will become as a speaker – and the more likely that your proposals will be listened to and acted on.

See also
Q1   What makes an effective speaker?
Q4   How can I identify and eliminate my weaknesses as a speaker?
Q5   What are my strengths as a speaker?
Q57   How can I build my confidence as a speaker?
Q88   Which personal attribute is essential to all presentations?
Q96   What should I reflect on when the presentation is over?

ABOUT THE AUTHOR

Author photo: Howard Baird

Elizabeth P. Tierney, PhD is a writer, trainer, consultant and lecturer in Communications and Management. She was a school administrator in the US and taught at University College Dublin, Ireland, Cesuga in Spain, and Willamette University in Oregon.

She coaches and delivers workshops, speaks at conferences and is the author of 14 books. Her latest, *Word Time! A Guide to Effective Writing,* a companion to *Show Time!,* was published by Oak Tree Press in 2023.